THE NATIONAL HOME MORTGAGE REDUCTION KIT

How To Cut Your Mortgage In Half & Own Your Home Free And Clear In Just A Few, Short Years.

By Benji O. Anosike, B.B.A.,M.A.,Ph.D.

Copyright © 2000 by Benji O. Anosike

Library of Congress Cataloging-in-Publication Data

Anosike, Benji O.
    The national home mortgage reduction kit : how to cut your mortgage in half & own
  your home free and clear in just a few, short years / by Benji O. Anosike.-- National ed.
      p. cm.
    " ... usable in all 50 states."
    Includes bibliographical references and index.
    ISBN 0-93270-442-5 (pbk. : alk. paper)
    1. Mortgage loans--United States. 2. Prepayment of debts--United States. I. Title.

HG2040.5.U5 A76 2000
332.7'22 21--dc21

                                         99-044611

Printed in the United States of America
ISBN: 0-932704-42-5

Library of Congress Catalog Number:

Published by:

Do-It-Yourself Legal Publishers
60 Park Place
Newark, NJ 07102

The Publisher's Disclaimer

Table of Contents

Chapter 4
WHY MORTGAGE ACCELERATION WILL GENERALLY BE A SOUND FINANCIAL INVESTMENT FOR THE AVERAGE HOMEOWNER

Chapter 5
SOME FEW SITUATIONS WHEN IT MAY NOT MAKE GOOD FINANCIAL SENSE TO ACCELERATE YOUR MORTGAGE PAYMENTS

Chapter 6
ACCELERATION PLANS FOR ADJUSTABLE RATE MORTGAGES

Chapter 7
OVERCOMING THE INHERENT 'DILEMMA' THAT'S INVOLVED IN DOING PAYMENT ACCELERATION: BEING ABLE TO AFFORD THE EXTRA PAYMENTS IT REQUIRES

Chapter 8
SOME DIFFERENT TYPES OF PRE-PAYMENT PLANS AVAILABLE. CHOOSING AN APPROPRIATE ONE FOR YOU

Chapter 9
TO DERIVE THE MAXIMUM BENEFITS FROM YOUR PREPAYMENT PROGRAM, YOU MUST PERSONALLY KEEP A CLOSE TRACK OF YOUR PAYMENTS

Chapter 10
PAYING OFF (ACCELERATING) YOUR MORTGAGE FAST & STEADY: HERE ARE THE COMPLETE STEP-BY-STEP PROCEDURES TO DO IT, FROM START TO FINISH

Chapter 11
REFINANCING YOUR MORTGAGE AS A SPECIAL TYPE OF MORTGAGE REDUCTION PLAN THAT CUTS DOWN YOUR INTEREST COSTS AS WELL

<u>APPENDICES</u>

INTRODUCTION

Why Paying Off Your Mortgage Ahead Of Schedule ("Acceleration"), Is The Primary Key To Your Getting Out Of The Dreaded American 'Debt Trap' Onto The Path To Excellent Financial Health

A. Which Would You Rather Pay For The Same Product: $100,000, or Two or Three Times That Amount?

Apparently directed to you, the homeowner or would-be homeowner, Michael C. Thomsett, a noted financial planner and home mortgage expert, puts his finger squarely on the central issue of this book, in a nutshell. Thomsett succinctly puts it this way: "When it comes to buying a house, the question might well be: 'Do you want to spend $100,000, or do you want to spend $270,000?' We would all answer $100,000. But if you settle for that [traditional] 30-year mortgage and don't accelerate, then, in fact, you are paying the higher amount."[*]

For you, the homeowner, the above proposition is, in a word, the central question posed by *The National Home Mortgage Reduction Kit* for you. Put another way, ***the basic question for you is: Would you, the prudent, rational, human being and family financial planner you are, who obviously work very hard for your money, rather pay $270,000 (or more) on a property, than merely $100,000!?***

Reduced to its most simplistic terms, this manual basically provides you, the homeowner and reader, the proven but tried-and-tested tools and techniques for mortgage reduction which would allow you to choose to pay the much lower price for the same house, rather than the higher price; the $100,000 price, instead of the $270,000—and at no particular extra expense or efforts on your part.

B. Getting Out Of The Crippling American Debt Trap Quickly Is Easy, Attainable & Desirable

Because it's often true that for most people, the biggest investment they'll ever make in their lives—and the biggest debt obligation they'll ever have—is often their homes, one vital key to getting out of debt is paying off your home mortgage ahead of schedule—that is, speeding up your mortgage payments ("acceleration") by paying off the mortgage early, ahead of schedule ("pre-payment"). Most people, unfortunately, are grossly unaware that they can actually pay off their home mortgage early, in fact many are not sure that it is even legal to do so. For most of us, it has simply been pounded into our consciousness and engraved in our collective thinking that it takes—it must take—20, 25 or 30 years to pay for a house. It is what one analyst has rightly called the American syndrome of the "mortgage trap"!

But wait a minute. Think, reconsider. Do things actually have to be this way? The resounding answer, is: NOT AT ALL! Indeed, quite the contrary is the case. The central message of this

---

[*] Thomsett, *Your Home Mortgage*, p. 130. Note that these figures are based on a $100,000 home with $20,000 down, 30-year mortgage on $80,000 at 10% interest rate.

manual is that, for you, the modern day homeowner, things do not have to be this way; that you do not have to lock in yourself in a 30-year mortgage, or wind up paying your lender hundreds of thousands of dollars EXTRA in unnecessary interest cost for your home. That, rather, not only is it practicable for you to pay off your home mortgage some 5, 10 or more years before the usual 20 to 30 year schedule, but that it is, in fact, highly desirable and in your OWN best financial interest for you to do so, and at the very earliest possible time. *This manual shows you, for example, that "affordability" of the extra payments you'd need to accelerate your mortgage is no object, and shows you the practical ways by which you can afford a pre-payment program of some sort ,whatever your financial circumstances.*

C. The Magical Engine That Powers The Book's Unique Tools Of Mortgage Reduction Strategies

The tools and strategies outlined in the manual are neither difficult to understand nor complex to implement; they are simply not widely known or commonly used by homeowners. Some cynics, noting the limited extent to which the tools and strategies are used by homeowners, have gone to the extent of charging some kind of conspiratorial collusion among lenders and banks to keep the formula "secret" and hidden from the public. Bankers, these cynics say, just can't be expected to tell homeowners about a formula that would, after all, allow homeowners to lop thousands of dollars in interest, and several years, off their mortgage! The formula is simple: it's based on the financial principle of PREPAYMENT OF PRINCIPAL—that is, making early payments of the PRINCIPAL (the amount you actually owe), or paying it (the principal) off ahead of the regular time table shown on your amortization schedule. Nevertheless, this underlying principle of prepayment of the PRINCIPAL amount, when placed in the hands of an informed homeowner, immediately becomes a simple but straightforward, disciplined, and powerful mortgage reduction strategy, one that will not only reduce your loan repayment period dramatically by a third or more, but save you tens and hundreds of thousands of dollars in unnecessary interest expenses. This, in turn, allows you to be mortgage debt-free by the time you retire, or even far much earlier.

The approach of the manual is simple. First, you are given an elementary, simple-to-follow, understanding of how mortgages work, reduced for you purely to the basic level where virtually anyone can comprehend and assimilate it. You are able to see for yourself, in the most vivid and graphic terms, why and how it is that by its very nature, traditional 25 or 30-year mortgage "amortization" process is intrinsically structured just so that it puts greater and greater interest receipts (profits) in the lender's pockets rather than in yours; why it is, thus, imperative that you urgently adopt a different financial plan that reverses the profit flow and channels it into YOUR OWN (the borrower's) pocket—the prepayment approach. Once stirred by this startling revelation and knowledge, not too widely known by many a homeowner, it's then only a short, easy step thereafter for the reader to jump at using the strategies outlined in the manual to achieve for himself the horrendous benefits of mortgage acceleration and reduction of his loan term and to save himself huge sums in interest costs.

D. Why You Not Only Should, But Must, Use This Manual And The Financial Tools It Provides You.

Let's just put it in the simplest of terms. Let's put it this way: there is absolutely no dispute about it, it's an established, fact that's universally acknowledged by all that on virtually any 30-year mortgage loan (on any at all!), you, as the borrower, will end up paying 2 to 3 times the loan amount you're lent in interest expense over the life of the loan. (For the figures on your specific case, for example, simple take a look at the computed figures in the 'Truth-in-lending Disclosure Statement' that your lender must have given you when you were granted your loan.)[*] Because of this truism, virtually all credible financial experts and planners are almost unanimous in their view that *because mortgages represent the largest single debt for most people or families, speeding up your mortgage debt requirement and paying it off as fast as possible, or as fast as you can afford to, is the essential key to getting out of the much dreaded American financial 'debt trap,' and for getting on to the path to solid financial health for the rest of one's life.*

Shaun Aghili, a mortgage loan author and credit expert and a California Certified Financial Planner (CFP), probably sums it up for most financial experts, this way: "A mortgage acceleration payment plan is undoubtedly one of the most important financial planning tools you have available to you to ensure a comfortable and worry-free retirement."

All agreed? O.K., then. And, can we further take the liberty to go ahead and make this assumption: that, as a homeowner, and as just plain, rational-thinking, red-blooded American, you would rather prefer that you pay, say, $100,000 on the same product (your hypothetical home), rather than, say $270,000 (or more)? Fair enough? That you'll rather rid yourself of the major crippling debt burden in your life, some 5, 10, or even 15 years sooner? And that you'll rather find yourself in a position where you can have substantial extra money to spend on vacations, to save for your children's education, to indulge in some little luxuries, and on your retirement?

Fair enough! Here, outlined for you, simply and comprehensibly, in *The National Home Mortgage Reduction Kit (How To Cut Your Mortgage In Half & Own Your Home Free And Clear In Just A Few, Short Years)*, are the sure-fire tools and knowledge for you to attain precisely these.

HOW MUCH DO YOU WANT TO PAY THE BANK? THAT'S THE BASIC ISSUE FOR YOU!

For instance, here's a comparison between 15-year and 30-year schedules for a $100,000 mortgage at 8 percent interest.

	15-YEAR MORTGAGE	30-YEAR MORTGAGE
Monthly payments ($)	955.65	733.76
Number of payments	180	360
Total paid during the term of the mortgage ($)	172,017.00	264,153.60
Principle paid ($)	100,000.00	100,000.00
Interest paid ($)	72,017.00	164,153.60

Table A-1. Comparison of 30-year mortgage with a 15-year mortgage at 8 percent interest.

Conclusion: On this $100,000 mortgage, you can cut your spending by more than $92,000 if you can pay $222 more each month.

---

[*] Note that, by federal law, every mortgage lender is required to furnish each borrower, in a disclosure statement, such facts and details particular to his/her loan—the amount financed, the cost of credit in terms of annual percentage rate (APR), the dollar amount the credit will cost, and the total amount the borrower will repay over the term of the loan. See also, Chapters 1 & 8 of the manual for other calculations, and for general discussions and practical illustrations of this.

Finally, true, the book and various illustrations in the book are ostensibly targeted almost exclusively towards mortgages. They represent, after all, the largest simple debt for most people or families. Fortunately, though, there's another great news about this which should be prominently noted; namely: you should know that the same principles outlined in this book directly apply just as well, to every other kind of borrowing you can think of. And, that you can—you should—use these some principles of making early principal payments outlined in the manual to cut down on the cost of your every other borrowing and save heavily, as well—on your auto loans, student loans, credit card debts, home improvement loans, etc. *By this, you take complete personal charge and control of your own financial future: No more will you be at the mercy of lenders, or even their computers; no more do you have to let anyone else dictate your financial future for you. Rather, it is now YOU who sets your own course and who ensures your own financial emancipation and success.*

Table A-2. Comparison of a 30-year mortgage with a 15-year mortgage at varying interest rates.

MONTHLY PAYMENTS: 30-YEAR MORTGAGE

RATE OF INTEREST	AMOUNT OF MORTGAGE ($)						
	70,000	75,000	80,000	85,000	90,000	95,000	100,000
6%	419.69	449.66	479.64	509.62	539.60	569.57	599.55
6.5%	442.45	474.05	505.65	537.26	568.86	600.46	632.07
7%	465.71	498.98	532.24	565.51	598.77	632.04	665.30
7.5%	489.45	524.41	559.37	594.33	629.29	664.25	699.21
8%	513.64	550.32	587.01	623.70	660.39	697.08	733.76
8.5%	538.24	576.69	615.13	653.58	692.02	730.47	768.91
9%	563.24	603.47	643.70	683.93	724.16	764.39	804.66
9.5%	588.60	630.64	672.68	714.73	756.77	798.81	840.85
10%	614.30	658.18	702.06	745.94	789.81	833.69	877.57
10.5%	640.32	686.05	731.79	777.53	823.27	869.00	914.74
11%	666.63	714.24	761.86	809.47	857.09	904.71	952.32
11.5%	693.20	742.72	792.23	841.75	891.26	940.78	990.29
12%	720.03	771.46	822.89	874.32	925.75	977.18	1,028.61

MONTHLY PAYMENTS: 15-YEAR MORTGAGE

RATE OF INTEREST	AMOUNT OF MORTGAGE ($)						
	70,000	75,000	80,000	85,000	90,000	95,000	100,000
6%	590.70	632.89	675.09	717.28	759.47	801.66	843.86
6.5%	609.78	653.30	696.89	740.44	784.08	827.55	871.11
7%	629.18	674.12	719.06	764.00	808.95	853.89	898.83
7.5%	648.91	695.26	741.61	787.98	834.31	880.66	927.01
8%	668.96	716.74	764.52	812.30	860.09	907.87	955.65
8.5%	689.32	738.55	787.79	837.03	886.27	935.50	984.74
9%	709.99	760.70	811.42	862.13	912.84	963.55	1,014.27

9.5%	730.96	783.17	835.38	887.59	939.80	992.01	1,044.22
10%	752.22	805.95	859.68	913.41	967.14	1,020.87	1,074.61
10.5%	773.78	829.05	884.32	939.59	994.86	1,050.13	1,105.40
11%	795.62	852.45	909.28	966.11	1,022.94	1,079.77	1,136.60
11.5%	817.73	876.14	934.55	992.96	1,051.37	1,109.78	1,168.19
12%	840.12	900.13	960.13	1,020.14	1,080.15	1,140.16	1,200.17

To figure out the total interest payable by you, find your monthly payment in the table. Then multiply by 360 (the number of months), for a 30-year mortgage, and by 180, for a 15-year mortgage. And subtract the principal, in either of the two cases. The difference is how much you'll save if you take a 15-year instead of a 30-year mortgage.

CHAPTER I
THE BASIC PRINCIPLES THAT APPLY IN ALL MORTGAGES: HOW MORTGAGES WORK

A. What Is A Mortgage?

If you really want to be technically correct about it, the "mortgage" is actually not the very loan that you, as a home buyer, take out to buy the property; it is, actually, the document, the legal agreement that you sign for the money's lender which gives the lender the right to the property (the right to "foreclose") in the event you "default" (i.e., fail) in repaying the loan. To put it another way, the MORTGAGE document is the instrument that creates a "lien" (a claim) on the borrower's property, which then makes it possible for it to serve as a _collateral_ to secure the promise of payment.

Throughout most of this book, however, when we use the term "_mortgage_", we will commonly think it to mean, as most people do, simply the MORTGAGE LOAN—the mortgage money with which the home purchase is generally made.

B. The Three Major Attributes Of A Mortgage – The Mortgage 'Big Three'

For our purposes in this manual, there are THREE basic attributes essential to a mortgage, each of which affects your home's ultimate cost to you.

They are: • the principal (amount)
   • the interest (rate)
   • the payment term (time).

The PRINCIPLE is the loan amount taken, the amount of money borrowed. The INTEREST is what you pay the lender for the use of its money. (interest plus principal, equals the total payment). And the payment TERM is the length (amount) of time it will take you to repay the mortgage.

C. How The Major Mortgage 'Big Three' Determine
Your Home's Ultimate Cost

Question: Generally speaking, when you think about a house in terms of its price and what it will cost for you to own it, what question immediately comes to your mind? Probably the purchase price issues about the house: 'What is its list price; will I be able to come up with the down payment? And will I be able to keep up the monthly payments on the mortgage?' Indeed, these, exactly, are what the average person who contemplates being a house owner basically thinks of as being the TOTAL cost of a house, as being all it will basically cost him (her) to own that dream house of his that he contemplates buying.

But, is that really the case? Is that really ALL it costs, or even most of what it costs, to own a house? NOT AT ALL! Not by any means. In truth, the hard reality concerning the buying and owning of a home is that the officially "contracted" costs of a house, such as the above mentioned costs, represent only a lesser fraction, a small portion, of the *actual* TOTAL COST of a house. The above mentioned costs do not even represent the larger part of a home's total cost. To put it simply, ***what will cost you far, far, more in the end in purchasing your home, are not the more immediate or near-term cost factors, like the home's list price, or the down payment amount for its purchase, and the like, but the "long-term" cost factors of buying the home.*** If you are like the average American home buyer, the overwhelming odds are that you probably will, of necessity, finance your home purchase with a lender's mortgage. And that'll mean that you will, in the end, have to pay not merely the house purchase price figure you were quoted by the house seller at the time of purchase, but probably ***two or three times more*** than that amount. You'll pay that primarily in the form of ***INTEREST***! (See the "ILLUSTRATION" below)

In other words, what you will wind up paying for your home will be determined by a combination of what we'll call the home mortgage 'Big Three'—the loan amount of your mortgage (principal); the interest rate of the loan; and the payment term or period. *The higher any one (or more) of these attributes is, the greater the amount of the TOTAL home cost you'll wind up paying in the end.* The total interest payment you'll pay on a $100,000 mortgage loan, will, for example, be much greater than what you'll pay on a $50,000 mortgage loan; the longer the term of the loan, the greater the <u>total</u> interest cost (though the lower the monthly payment you'll need to pay); and the higher the interest rate, the greater the total loan amount you pay in the end.

ILLUSTRATION. To give you an idea of this reality about the impact of the mortgage 'Big Three,' let's use just one element of the Big Three factors, the 'interest factor,' to illustrate how much you are actually going to wind up paying on a given home purchase. We'll use something called an INTEREST FACTOR TABLE—Figure 1-1 below. Designed for a standard 30-year, fixed rate mortgage, this table allows you to compute the total interest charges you are to pay out over the term of your mortgage loan. You simply multiply the loan amount with the "interest factor" applicable to your mortgage interest rate. Thus, let's say you're buying a home worth $200,000, and that you put 10% of that as down payment and borrowed the remainder (i.e., $180,000) at 9.75 percent fixed rate of interest for a 30-year term. Now, using the interest factor from Table 1-1 for 9.75%, you can determine that you'll pay $180,000 x 2.093 or $376,740 in total interest cost (the interest alone) over the 30-year life of the mortgage. Now, this represents the INTEREST COST only. To determine the total cost of the mortgage, you now add this interest cost to the amount borrowed $376,740 + $180,000), and to determine the TOTAL COST[*] of the home to you, you further have to add the amount of the down payment you had put down on the home, making it $376,740 + $180,000 + $20,000 or $576,740.*

---

[*] This figure does not include all and every conceivable costs, obviously, costs such as insurance or real property taxes, home improvement or repair and maintenance costs, and the like.

Figure 1-1. Selected Interest Factors Table For Loans

7% = 1.395	10.5 = 2.293	14 = 3.266
7.25 = 1.456	10.75 = 2.361	14.25 = 3.337
7.5 = 1.517	11 = 2.428	14.5 = 3.408
7.75 = 1.579	11.25 = 2.497	14.75 = 3.480
8 = 1.642	11.5 = 2.565	15 = 3.552
8.25 = 1.705	11.75 = 2.634	15.25 = 3.624
8.5 = 1.768	12 = 2.703	15.5 = 3.696
8.75 = 1.832	12.25 = 2.772	15.75 = 3.769
9 = 1.897	12.5 = 2.842	16 = 3.841
9.25 = 1.962	12.75 = 2.912	16.25 = 3.914
9.5 = 2.027	13 = 2.982	16.5 = 3.987
9.75 = 2.093	13.25 = 3.053	16.75 = 4.059
10 = 2.159	13.5 = 3.124	17 = 4.132
10.25 = 2.226	13.75 = 3.194	17.25 = 4.206

Here's the simple formula for this:

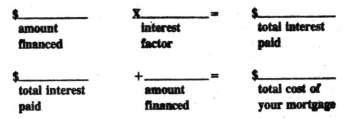

$\underline{\hspace{2cm}}$	X$\underline{\hspace{2cm}}$ =	$\underline{\hspace{2cm}}$
amount financed	interest factor	total interest paid
$\underline{\hspace{2cm}}$	+$\underline{\hspace{2cm}}$ =	$\underline{\hspace{2cm}}$
total interest paid	amount financed	total cost of your mortgage

($ amount financed) × (interest factor) = $ total interest paid

($ total interest paid) + ($ amount borrowed) = $ total of your loan

$ total of your loan + your down payment = total direct cost of the house

D. The Basic Strategy Behind Mortgage Pre-Payment Or Acceleration

Looking at the above-described scenario slightly differently, in terms of doing some strategic financial planning, what this means is that if you can find a way by which to effect a change, downwards, in just one (or more) of these BIG THREE factors of your mortgage, you would have correspondingly effected a change, also downwards, on your home's ultimate cost. *In a word, that, precisely, is what mortgage repayment acceleration program is simply all about.* Mortgage acceleration, because it eliminates part of the loan term, which is indeed the most significant among the three main attributes, directly reduces your interest cost, and you are thus able not only to determine the amount of debt you owe and to reduce the amount of debt you owe, but also to determine the future date on which you will own your home debt-free and clear.

PAY MORE NOW, SAVE A LOT MORE LATER

Even if you have to pay more money each month, the key to saving on your mortgage in the long run is to pay for as few months as possible. Here's a comparison of your total costs on a typical $100,000 loan at 10 percent interest rate

TABLE 1.2 *Impact of the Loan Term*

Monthly payments and total interest payments for a basic $100,000 fixed-rate mortgage loan at 10 percent interest

Length of Loan	Monthly Payment	Total Interest Paid
15 years	$1,074.61	$ 93,430
20 years	965.02	131,605
25 years	908.70	172,610
30 years	877.57	215,925

Figure 1-2. The Impact of The Length of Time Taken In Paying Off a Loan

E. Loan Amortization And The Basic Lesson To Learn From Amortization

The term "amortization" refers to the gradual, systematic liquidation or repayment of a debt through normal, regular payments. Indeed, interestingly, the term is directly derived from a Latin word meaning "deadening"—denoting the gradual killing off of a debt for the benefit of the lender!

In various sections of this manual (see pp.1-3, for example), we have attempted to show in any number of ways, the high cost of financing a house through the loan "amortization" or normal mortgage repayment method, and how *the bulk of the interest income, equity, and profits that result from owning a house predominantly go to or accrue to the benefit of the lender relative to the homeowner.* One of the best ways of demonstrating, as well as understanding, this fact—and of thus showing the crucial need for the homeowner to engage in mortgage acceleration in order to remedy that problem—is to analyze the typical mortgage amortization process, and to track it and observe just how fast, or how slowly, the mortgage loan typically gets paid off. By simply tracking closely the loan amortization process and analyzing it, we are able to see quite clearly just how much of the payment go for INTEREST and how much towards reducing the loan debt itself, and at what speed and to whose benefit, the homeowner's or the lender's.

F. The Amortization Or Loan Repayment Process—How It Really Works

Suppose that, as an 'average Joe' with no special expertise or knowledge in these matters, you merely are interested in getting a rough idea of how the amortization of a mortgage will work out, say on a $100,000 loan at an interest rate of 10 percent for the standard 30 year term? Just off hand, what you might probably think is that you'd probably pay $10,000 in interest for the loan (10 percent of the $100,000 principal), plus 1/30th of the principal, or $3,333. That's seemingly logical, isn't it!? So it might seem. But it's also all wrong. Loans simply aren't structured that way!

Rather, loans are structured in a drastically different way. Most repayment plans ("amortization") would call for a series of regular, equal monthly payments. Each monthly payment is applied, first to pay the INTEREST which has accrued, and the remainder then to pay the outstanding PRINCIPAL. Thus, in the typical long-term loan (15 to 30 years), the payments will be divided into either 180 or 360 monthly payments.

BUT HERE'S THE IMPORTANT POINT FOR YOU TO NOTE: because of the special way loans are structured, *in the EARLIER years of the mortgage term, most of the mortgage payments (those equal monthly payments) you make consist almost entirely of INTEREST, with the loan PRINCIPAL left virtually untouched. Only many, many years down the road, after you shall have already made a large amount of payments to the lender with virtually all of it being credited to INTEREST (his profit), will a slowly increasing share of each payment that you make begin to go toward paying the* principal. Then, month by month, gradually, you pay more of the principal and less of the interest, until, toward the end, your payments become mostly principal.

To put it another way, mortgage loan amortizations are structured in a unique way; they are structured in such a way that when your loan balance (the actual amount you still owe) is high, more of each monthly payment you make goes to INTEREST (the lender's profit) and only a small amount goes toward the loan itself (the principal). The interest (the lender's profit) on the loan is said to be "front-end loaded,"—that is, paid first upfront to the lender *before* the principal begins to be paid. Consequently, because of the nature of the mortgage loan structure—because the amount of interest chargeable on a loan is figured based on the remaining loan balance, meaning the amount of the loan still unpaid—the loan balances (the amount still owed or unpaid) decline only very, very *slowly*, indeed painfully so.

To illustrate, let us track a typical 30-year mortgage; as we do, just notice closely how excruciatingly *slow* the loan is paid down, how slowly the balances (what is still owed or unpaid) actually decrease over long stretches of time.

Look at the monthly payment schedule, known as "Amortization Schedule," shown below in Figure 1-3—for a mortgage of $100,000 amortized (i.e., paid off) over a 30 year term, at 10 percent interest.* The payment over the 30 year period is $877.57 per month, each divided between what goes towards paying the "principal" (the specific amount you actually borrowed), and what goes towards paying the "interest" (the lender's profit for lending you the money). As you can see from Figure 1-3 below, each month's payment ($877.57) always breaks down to two parts: between the INTEREST and the PRICIPAL. For example, the very first month's payment of $877.57 breaks down as follows: Principal $44.24, and Interest $833.33, for the combined total of the $877.57 per month. Thus, Figure 1-3's Amortization Schedule shows how payments on a $100,000, 30-year term, 10 percent loan, breaks down each month—in interest, principal, and the balance—for the 30 year duration of the loan period. [See, also, Figure 5-1 on p.15 for precisely the same picture]

---

* When your mortgage loan is issued, your lender will often give you an Amortization Schedule or Table, which will show you, month-to-month, the principal and interest payments and the declining balance. You also can get such a table from your real estate agent or from a prospective lender.

Figure 1-2. Sample Amortization Table
30-year, $100,000 Mortgage at 10 Percent

Month	Starting Balance	Payment Principal	Interest	Ending Balance
1	$100,000.00	$44.24	$833.33	$99,955.76
2	99,955.76	44.61	832.96	99,911.16
3	99,911.16	44.98	832.59	99,866.18
4	99,866.18	45.35	832.22	99,820.84
5	99,820.84	45.73	831.84	99,775.12
6	99,775.12	46.11	831.46	99,729.02
7	99,729.02	46.49	831.08	99,682.52
8	99,682.52	46.88	830.69	99,635.64
9	99,635.64	47.27	830.30	99,588.38
10	99,588.38	47.67	829.90	99,540.72
↓	↓	↓	↓	↓
351	8,394.96	807.61	69.96	7,587.35
352	7,587.35	814.34	63.23	6,773.01
353	6,773.01	821.13	56.44	5,951.88
354	5,951.88	827.97	46.90	5,123.91
355	5,123.91	834.87	42.70	4,289.04
356	4,289.04	841.83	35.74	3,447.21
357	3,447.21	848.84	28.73	2,598.37
358	2,598.37	855.92	21.65	1,742.45
359	1,742.45	863.05	14.52	870.24
360	870.24	870.24	7.33	-0-

As you can clearly see for yourself, the following facts can immediately be gleaned from this scrutiny:

FIRSTLY: That the EARLIER YEARS of the loan, when the borrower's loan balance is high, is when MORE of the borrower's payments go to INTEREST, while a SMALL AMOUNT goes toward the PRINCIPAL (the loan itself). For example, in the first month's payment in the table, while the interest (the lender's profit) is a whopping $833.33, only a pitiful $44.24 is for the principal, the actual amount that's applied towards reducing the debt.

SECOND: That in the LATER years of the loan, when the borrower's loan balance is low (or lower), there is a complete switch: gradually, MORE of the borrower's payments now go to the PRINCIPAL, and smaller and SMALLER AMOUNTS go to INTEREST. For example, while the interest part in the first month of payment in Table 1-3 is a whopping $833.33, in the 351st month the interest part is way down to only $69.96, and by the 359th month, it a meager $14.52. But, on the other hand, by the 351st month a staggering $807.61 of the borrower's payment now goes to liquidating the principal (the actual debt), and in the 359th month, it's up to $863.05—up from a measly $44.24 in the first month!

THIRDLY: That in the EARLIER years of the mortgage, the borrower's loan balances (the amount still owed) decline very, very slowly, if barely, while in the LATER years there is a switch: the balances decline in that period in ever GREATER amounts each month, and do so more rapidly.[*] For example, as can be seen from Table 1-B, upon making the 1st month's payment of $877.57 (interest plus principal), the loan balance only declines to $99,955.76, and by the 10th month's payment, with a total of $8,775.70 already paid in by then, the loan balance has barely moved, declining to only $99,540.72—a decline of just $459.28. But now, in contrast, take a look at the comparable LAST 10 payments of the mortgage; and you'll find, on the other hand, a dramatic and rapid decline in the loan balance: the drop in the balance in the one month period from the 351st to 352nd month, for example, is a steep $807.61, and in the very last one month period, the 360th month, it is a gigantic drop of $870.24

Indeed, on this loan, as in the average 30-year mortgage, at the end of the 10th year, just when you are at the one-third mark of the loan term, only 9 percent of the total loan shall have been paid off. Out of the $100,000 loaned you, you will still be owing about $90,000 to your lender at that point, after 10 years. In fact, by the middle of the 24th year, all you shall have paid off is only one-half of the loan, and only in the last 6 years of the 30 year term will you pay off the second one-half![*]

THE MAJOR IMPLICATION: The reality is clear that, in the amortization process, in the EARLY years each payment you make consists almost entirely of INTEREST that accrues solely to your lender's benefit, and that it is only towards the ENDING part of the loan term that the payments largely begin to go to the PRINCIPAL for the actual paying down of your loan, thereby strongly suggesting two things: (1) the need for some acceleration (speeding up) of the payment process by the borrower; and (2) that the earlier the borrower can begin such a program of additional or increased payment on his (her) mortgage, the greater the financial benefit it will yield for him.

G. The Magical Power of "Compound" Interest & the Effect of Accelerating Or Pre-Paying Your Mortgage

What is the investment value of pre-paying or making a payment acceleration of a mortgage? (To "accelerate" simply means speeding up your payments so that you pay off your mortgage in less time than your loan term stipulates.) What, for example, is the investment value to you of paying an EXTRA $100 per month towards your mortgage?

In the author's experience, generally speaking no matter how many times or in how many ways you explain this to individuals, it seemingly remains mystifying, mystifying not only in regard to how the pre-payment of principal process really works, but even more importantly, in terms of how such a seemingly simple factor could have such a dramatic effect on the total, overall cost of borrowing. Most people cannot comprehend (or get themselves to believe), for example, just

---

[*] Indeed, the reason why this is so is simple. In the earlier years, since it is on the still outstanding balance of a loan that the interest chargeable is figured, much of the payment that is made will necessarily have to go towards interest, and not to the loan itself!

[*] As a rule, the two major parts of the mortgage payment, the principal and interest, do not even get to equal each other in amount until halfway through the term of the loan. Before the halfway point (15 years on a 30 year loan), more money goes to paying the interest than it does to paying the principal. After the halfway point, the greater amount now goes towards the principal and lesser amount goes toward interest. In sum, the central point is this: that the far larger share of the amount of money you pay monthly on the first half of your mortgage is INTEREST—i.e., PROFIT TO YOUR BANK OR LENDER!

how all the payments under a $100,000, 30-year mortgage at 10% interest, could amount to $315,925 in total cost to the borrower. Or, that payments for the same loan amount at the same interest rate where you choose to go with a 15-year term, instead of 30 years, would amount to so much less in total cost, some $193,450 less.

Actually, however, the underlying principle behind the prepayment of the loan principal is not at all difficult to understand. In the most simple term, all you need do is understand one basic concept on which bankers and lenders have for ages built their empires: *the concept of COMPOUND INTEREST and how it works.*

In a word, Compound Interest is simply interest earned on interest. Let's say you leave $100 (the principal) in a savings account at a 10 percent interest rate for a period of one year. At the end of the first year, your $100 deposit (the principal) shall have earned $10 in interest, meaning that you now have in the account a total of $110 ($100 + $10). Now, if you leave both amounts (the original principal and the earned interest) in the account and do not withdraw the earned interest ($10), then in the next period that $10 (interest), as well, will earn its own interest of $1 (10% on $10), and so on and on. This process will continue in each successive period. In other words, the interest you earn is now computed not just on the principal (the original $100), but on the principal as well as the interest amounts, and each year interest is earned on the ever growing principal. When this process is repeated for each successive period, there is felt the "compounded" power and effect of the compound interest.

By the same token, the same very compound interest principle applies in loan payment in reverse. When you borrow money from a bank, it is on the _outstanding balance_ of your loan that the bank computes the interest due it. And because it is on the outstanding balance that the interest is figured, the interest cost in the EARLIER years of your mortgage term is much greater than it is later on. What this phenomenon of a gradual swing from high INTEREST payments (i.e. cost to you) in the early years, to higher PRINCIPAL payments (i.e., savings to you) during the later years, implies for you as a borrower, is very, very profound in deed. Simply put, what it implies for you as a borrower is that *if by some mechanism you were to be able to eliminate a part of the OUTSTANDING BALANCE on your loan for a given month or period, that would mean that that's one part you would not have to pay interest on as from that point in time; you would save yourself that much interest cost.* IN OTHER WORDS, IT SUGGESTS A GREAT NEED FOR, AND AN ADVANTAGE OF, MORTGAGE PAYMENT ACCELERATION: THE SOONER YOU BEGIN A PROGRAM FOR ADDITIONAL PAYMENTS ON YOUR MORTGAGE, THE LOWER YOUR OVERALL COSTS. What is significant to recognize is this: on a loan bearing interest charge at 10 percent, for example, for every amount, say $100, by which you reduce your loan balance today, you will earn an equivalent 10 percent of it for the remainder of the loan term, through reducing the cost of repayment. Thus, if, for example, on a mortgage that bears 10 percent interest rate you were to eliminate (reduce) your loan balance today by, say, $100, or $1000, $5000, or whatever the sum, that act, for you, is directly equivalent to your earning 10 percent of that given amount for the entire remainder of the loan term—you shall have, in effect, eliminated the cost of repayment (the interest cost) on that $100, $1,000, or $5,000 amount, month after month, for the remaining term of the loan, and thus "earning" it. In other words, by simply "pre-paying" a loan—making payment of a set amount in advance, before it's due—you are saving (or, conversely, you are earning) yourself all the compound interest that the bank would have collected on that prepaid amount for the remaining duration of that loan! Take, for example, an $80,000 mortgage for illustrative purposes, as shown in Figure 1-4 below. As shown in Figure 1-4, assuming monthly compounding of interest at 10 percent (in the same way that your bankers will figure your mortgage interest to them), for every $100 reduction (pre-payment) you are able to make on your loan balance today, you earn (save) yourself, $1,984 in interest over the 30-year term—the reduced cost of repayment on a $100 loan amount which you do not now have to pay. [See Table 1-4 below]. That will amount to getting a saving (reduction) in total interest costs of almost three months payments (at $702.06 each) for just adding a one-time $100 extra in the very first month's payment. And, as you can see from Table 1-4, the longer the loan term on which the prepayment is to be made, or the higher the rate of interest or of the loan balance, the higher the savings to you. Thus, if your mortgage is for a 20 year term, or you have 20 years still to go on your mortgage, for example, every $100 prepayment you make today will yield you $733 over the 20 year term.

Here's the effect of prepaying $100, one time only, at various interest rates for different terms:

YEARS	MORTGAGE INTEREST RATE			
	8%	10%	12%	14%
5	$ 149	$ 165	$ 182	$ 201
10	222	271	330	402
15	331	445	600	807
20	493	733	1,089	1,618
25	734	1,206	1,979	3,245
30	1,094	1,984	3,595	6,506

Figure 1-4: value of $100 prepayment on an $80,000 loan at different interest rates.

IMPORTANT: Notice the real mechanical engine behind this seemingly magical effect: the magic of the compound interest principle. A one-time-only payment (the $100) benefits you in two "compound" ways: by reducing the interest you'll have to pay, first in the following month, and then for every month still remaining in your loan term (through the lowering of the loan balances, the PRINCIPAL, by the same $100 for every future month). (That interest you would have incurred is now reduced to you because, the one-time $100 extra payment is directly applied to the loan balance— the PRINCIPAL—to reduce it, thus completely eliminating it for good for the rest of the loan term.) The benefit of this one-time payment to you, as a borrower, is literally 'compounded' in that each time you make your monthly payment, the interest you'll be charged on that will be computed on the loan balance LESS the $100.

STRATEGY

GET RID OF EXCESS DEBT !

CHAPTER 2
BEFORE ANY MORTGAGE ACCELERATION, ONE KEY PREREQUISITE YOU MUST FIRST HAVE IN PLACE: SET UP AN EMERGENCY RESERVE FUND

Elsewhere in this guidebook, namely in Chapter 5, it is fairly well established that for a given acceleration plan to work, it must, first and foremost, be one that is _practical_ in terms of being something you can realistically afford in terms of your budget. The central point of that chapter is simple, namely, that even the best financial plan in the world will work ONLY IF the money required for its fulfillment is there, and that, as a first prerequisite if you can't afford accelerating your mortgage payment today, then you simply must wait till you can and should not prematurely jump into it. In this chapter, we shall explore yet another key prerequisite you should have in place before you may embark on a plan of acceleration: HAVING AN EMERGENCY RESERVE FUND of available cash in place.

A. Why You Need This Fund

Financial planners generally advise that, ideally, a family (or homeowner) contemplating implementing a plan of mortgage acceleration, should attempt to begin by FIRST establishing a separate savings fund of liquid cash or cash equivalents BEFORE he may wisely embark on such a program. For any family, having some liquid reserve of money set aside and readily available to be used in the event of emergencies, is something that almost always makes great sense, in any event. More specifically, however, for the homeowner who is intending to accelerate his mortgage payment, the point of having an emergency reserve fund _**in advance**_ of that, is to have a protective cushion in the event of sudden, unanticipated and unbudgeted expenses or needs. Briefly stated, the general informed view is that in the long run, for any program of sustained, accelerated mortgage payment to work, the periodic payment you make on your mortgage per month or period, must not be so high that you do not have some reasonable savings or extras still left over to meet some periodic emergencies. Or, to put it another way, you should postpone it rather than rush to pay off your mortgage, if, for example, it will leave your savings and investments so totally depleted that you might suffer grave financial inconvenience or hardship if the roof should leak or your car should need a new tire, or if you will not be able continuously to meet your vital obligations, such as a college tuition expenditure, property taxes or insurance, a new or replacement car purchase, etc.

As a realistic, practical matter, there are several possible emergencies that may arise in your life as a home-owner: sudden or unanticipated loss of job, a prospect not particularly too remove in the modern American era of pervasive "downsizing"; sudden car repairs, hospital and health emergency bills, and home maintenance. And, in addition, there is always the prospect in the life of a family that certain large expenditure items may at some point arise—college tuition, a vacation, a family wedding, a new car purchase, etc.

Obviously, your existing family budget will be hard hit if such extraordinary expenses were suddenly to arise. Suppose you were to run into a severe emergency situation. Let's say you lose your job, for example, and that your income unexpectedly ceases. In such a situation a reserve fund of some sort, if available, will come in handy for you just to meet your normal expenses until you can, perhaps, resume working again. If you are fortunate—especially when you have built up good equity in the property, or can boast of a solid record of past repayment of your other debts and a strong credit rating—you'll probably be able to persuade your mortgage lenders to allow you a grace period and to suspend your monthly payments for some 3 to 6 months. As a rule, most lenders would rather work with you than end up having to recover from you, and then sell, the property in an often protracted and expensive legal procedure called "foreclosure". Not all lenders, though, will be patient and understanding, or willing to work with you under those circumstances. Suppose your mortgage lender is the inflexible type who will still insist on continued timely payments and threaten legal action and foreclosure if you were to fail to comply? Here will, again, be the type of circumstance where having an emergency reserve fund will be highly essential and useful. *The point is that if you are already paying up to the hilt and have nothing left over after you make the regular mortgage and family expenses, then it would surely be a serious financial strain for you, and you run a grave risk of not finding money to meet any emergencies under such circumstances—unless, of course, you shall have set aside some money in a reserve designed to meet such emergencies.*

The case for setting up a reserve fund as a PREREQUISITE for accelerating your mortgage payments, is made all the more stronger by this fundamental fact: the mortgage fund is an extremely illiquid investment. That is, you can't convert the mortgage payment to cash or get your money back easily once you invest it in the mortgage payment since it's not readily available for immediate use once invested. It's not like a passbook savings account or mutual fund which are considered a highly liquid type of asset or investment that can be readily "cashed in" for dollars virtually on demand. For a real property type of investment, once the investment is made the only way you may recoup money from it after that, would be by way of borrowing against it (still another debt!) or by selling it.

In contrast to that, however, an emergency reserve fund provides that kind of needed liquid asset that can immediately be put to use. Hence, the common advice by experts that before you ever start a mortgage acceleration program and put additional money into your home equity and mortgage payments—an investment which, by its very nature is a very illiquid one that is not readily available once made—you had better established a fairly reasonable liquid reserve fund of cash that will be readily available at a moment's notice for you to fall back on in the event of an emergency or unanticipated cash need.

B. Nature Of The Reserve Fund

How much should you set aside as "adequate" reserve amount? There are different opinions about this among financial planners. But, generally, the most common figure suggested among them, is a savings cushion of three to six months' take-home pay. In the final analysis, however, after all it said and done a lot will still depend on your income level, and on such basic factors as whether you have one working spouse or two in the family, the size and level of monthly expenses that apply in your particular case for necessities and recurring payments in your family budget, and the good, old, ability-to-save on your own part. Furthermore, aside from your home equity and the emergency reserve fund you set up, you should presumably have had other liquid or semi liquid investments as well in your overall financial plan, fully diversified (stocks, mutual funds, savings bonds, etc.), as diversification is commonly agreed by financial experts to be an absolute essential for any sound investment plan.

The reserve fund should be set up in a form which lends itself to being drawn out in "liquid" (cash) form in the quickest possible way—a passbook savings account in a secure, federally insured, local bank or other similarly sound financial institutions, for example, or an account with a so-called "no-load" money market mutual fund which invests in special financial instruments like short-term government and corporate notes or certificates of deposit and bankers acceptances, as such funds can be withdrawn in the same way that a customer can with a checking account by simply writing a check and cashing it.

An ideal way to be able to establish a reserve fund is to start out by setting aside a reasonable amount of money in your budget. To make it as painless and assured as possible, the amount you set aside must be a figure that is reasonably affordable so as to assure that you can make the deposits continuously over a long term without fail. Each month or paycheck, you first "pay yourself"—that is, you set aside a designated amount (say, 5 or 10 percent of the paycheck) and put it into a savings or mutual funds account, and budget your other expenses with what is left over. To be effective, however, the set aside and savings program must be done under conditions of strict and absolute discipline; once begun, you must stick with it, you must do it on a regular and continuous basis, making the set aside automatically each and every month or paycheck, and you must doggedly resist every temptation to withdraw from the fund—except, of course, in a real absolute emergency.

C. Ideal Level Of An Emergency Reserve Fund

What is the ideal level for an emergency reserve fund?   As has been emphasized in the preceding section, having an emergency reserve fund established and in place, should generally take first precedence over starting a plan of mortgage acceleration, though it is urgent, as well, that an acceleration be started at the earliest possible time. *Why? Because, as has been more elaborately emphasized elsewhere (See Section F Chapter 1) by the very way loan amortizations are structured, the earlier an amortization acceleration begins, and the greater the rate of amortization during such earlier years, the lower the overall minimum balance that will be required in the continued amortization of the loan, and the greater the financial benefits to you.*

Hence, in setting up an emergency reserve fund, the most ideal way to go about it is to set it up IN COORDINATION WITH an acceleration plan for reducing the overall cost of the house in the long run. Here, you are simply to treat the reserve fund as just one vital component in an overall "diversified" investment plan where the reserve fund is coordinated with other vital components, such as mutual funds, shares of stock, saving bonds, etc. The point is that establishing an emergency reserve fund and starting a mortgage acceleration program at the earliest possible time, do not necessarily conflict with each other, nor are they mutually exclusive; you need not necessarily have to select one over the other. Rather, you can have BOTH, more or less, at the same time.

How? By taking, simply, a balanced approach to the plan. For example, you can begin the acceleration of your mortgage at the same time that you establish an emergency reserve, but undertake the acceleration only modestly, until you can accumulate an adequate reserve. For instance, let's say that all you have available in your budget for both acceleration and setting up a savings reserve fund is a total of $100 per month. You can start both an emergency reserve fund and a modest mortgage acceleration plan at the same time and coordinate them this way: you put, say, $75 of that into the emergency reserve, and only $25 into acceleration. You build up the fund gradually over several years, and after some years when your reserve is adequately established, 100 percent of that extra money ($100) can now be put into the acceleration plan.

Both programs can be reasonably coordinated in the manner shown in Figure 2-1 below. During the first year, the entire extra $100 per month that's available for prepayment is allotted to the emergency reserve fund, for a total of $100. Then, the second year and each year thereafter, the emergency reserve fund allotment is reduced by $25 per month as the allotment to the mortgage acceleration is increased. Thus, in the second year of this sample, for example, $75 per month goes towards the emergency reserve fund and $25 goes towards mortgage acceleration; in the third year, it's $50 per month to the emergency reserve and $50 to mortgage acceleration. And so on. By the fifth year, the entire $100 per month now goes to mortgage acceleration payments, and at the end of that year an emergency reserve fund of $3,000 shall have been created.

Payments Made To Reserve Fund & Prepayment, From Year to Year:

Year	Reserve Fund	Mortgage
1	$1,200.	$0
2	900.	300.
3	600.	600.
4	300.	900.
5 and on	0.	1,200.

**Figure 2-1. Reserve Fund coordinated with mortgage acceleration program
@ $100 per month**

By having a coordinated approach to this whereby you simultaneously establish at the earliest possible time a reasonable level of reserve fund while moderately accelerating at the same time your mortgage payments, you'll enjoy the greater benefits (savings in interest over the term of the loan) from starting an acceleration plan early, and also reduce your risk factor through establishing a protection fund against an emergency. Of course, if, on the other hand, you are in a good financial situation requiring that you establish the emergency reserve fund first and then begin the mortgage acceleration next—if you possess the financial ability to pay, or you are at great risk, say, because, you are the sole breadwinner in the family and can't afford a potential loss of some 3 months income—then that's a standing alternative you may have to consider. Under such circumstance, it may probably be better to build up the reserve fund completely, before doing any acceleration at all.

CHAPTER 3
SOME COMMON MYTHS AND FLAWED ARGUMENTS RELATING TO MORTGAGE FINANCING, MORTGAGE PREPAYMENTS OR ACCELERATION

Some financial analysts have noted that, notwithstanding the general view common among most investment professionals, as well as the public alike, that paying down one's mortgage at the fastest possible pace is by and large a wise, and financially advantageous move for the homeowner, there are still many pockets of people—mostly mortgage lenders and real estate salespeople—who still insist that speeding up the mortgage repayment is an unwise financial idea. Such persons, these analysts say, have been largely able to sustain their "flawed" arguments against speedier loan repayment based on some popular "myths".

In Section A below, we outline the major arguments (myths) advanced by such persons who argue against everything from paying down the mortgage more speedily, to investing in real estate relative to other types of investments, and explore the merits of such arguments, if any. And in Section B, we shall examine the underlying purposes and motivations that often undergird such myths and arguments for those who frequently champion them.

A. The Principal Myths & Arguments

Among the major myths and arguments connected with home owning and financing, are the following:

MYTH #1: *That The Purchase Price Of The Home Is The True "Cost" Of The Property*

This is false. In reality, it is the amount of INTEREST you pay on the house financing over the years that more significantly represent the actual TOTAL cost of the property. For just one simple example, a $100,000 mortgage on a house paid off at 10 percent interest over 30 years, costs $215,925 in interest alone—plus the $100,000 that was supposed to be the purchase price!

MYTH #2: *That Equity In A Home Is Built Mainly From Increases In Market Value, Due To Demand For Housing*

A common attitude and assumption among many, is that the build-up of equity in a home comes about as a somewhat natural and automatic result of increased market value, combined with the gradual repayment of the mortgage loan. Many assume that housing is invariably a sound and profitable investment, and that housing prices would inevitably climb upwards over the years as a result of greater demand and increased equity in the property, and hence if you were to buy a house today and sell it 10 or even 5 years from today, you would almost surely sell it at a profit. With others, the assumption is common that major home improvements in a property will inevitably translate into a rise in the house's value and equity.

This attitude, however, which is dubbed the "passive" approach by one writer, is not only untrue but also often costly for the homeowner, as it invariably results in the mortgage lender earning a greater profit on the home than the homeowner or seller. True, home values increase as a result of demand, and housing prices in your area may well climb upwards. But there's no guarantee of that. Why? For this simple reason: increased demand is only one factor among many different variables which, together, combine to determine future value. Many other market and economic factors—the location of your home, the cost and level of care and maintenance you and your neighbors put into the property, the trends in crime rates or employment in the area, the state of the national economy or of your state's or region's economy, etc—have a great deal to do, as well, in determining the future value and equity for a house. And while home improvements made in one's property is almost always a sound investment, the assumption that your house's value and equity will rise dramatically or automatically as a result of that, is not always a safe one.

But here's another point: even if the equity and market value of your home were to substantially increase, there still will remain another important question for you, the question of WHO WILL PROFIT FROM THE INCREASE? One way of finding an answer to this question is by comparing the historical changes in housing prices to the cost of buying and borrowing. A homeowner's equity in a home, almost everyone agrees, builds up through reducing the mortgage debt on the house. But as you have learned in the previous chapters (see for example, Chapter 1, Sections F & G), for a house involving the typical 30-year mortgage term, for example, that kind of equity typically accumulates very slowly in the early years of the repayment term, in that in the early years of a mortgage each payment consists almost entirely of interest and it is only as time goes on that you begin to pay more of the principal and less of the interest until, toward the end when your payments become mostly principal. [See Figure 1-2, Sample Amortization Table on page 9, AND Figure 1-5 and p. 15]. Hence, for the homeowner, realistically the likelihood of having a substantial profit is low when you sell after only 5 to 10 years.

In sum, in the first place, while home values may increase over time as a result of demand and market forces, there are simply no guarantees that this will necessarily happen with your property. The amount of equity you will build in your home as a result of market conditions and home improvements, is simply both limited and uncertain, and, in any event, ultimately you are at the mercy of prevailing market and economic conditions and will have little control over the demand for or price of your property. Furthermore, even if the market value of the property increases considerably over the years that you own your home, the interest you pay your mortgage lender will offset that market value and hence you'll wind up making much less profit from buying the home than the lender makes, as much of that increased value is converted to profits not for you, but for the lender.

Housing experts have observed, for example, that no matter how much home improvements homesellers make on their houses to make them more attractive to potential buyers, the maximum sale price they obtain is often limited still, in that buyers are frequently not willing to pay a price substantially above that of comparable homes and such homes will usually not sell for an amount equal to the total cost of improvements just because you have added some value to the property.

MYTH #3: That You're Better Off Paying Full Interest On Your Mortgage Rather Than To Accelerate Payment, In That Acceleration Reduces The Tax Benefits Of Mortgage Interest Deduction.

Not quite so, however. True, mortgage interest is generally fully tax- deductible and you do reduce itemized deductions quite alright by accelerating your mortgage payments. However, this deduction is offset by the greater savings you make in overall costs. To put it another way, the fact is that even with the reduced deductions of your mortgage interest expenses on your tax return, you will still come out much farther ahead in the interest savings you make by accelerating, relative to what you lose by not taking the full itemized deductions (or what you would have gained if you had taken the full deduction).

Furthermore, for a lot of people the tax deduction doesn't mean very much. According to experts who have made the calculation,[*] depending on your tax bracket, each $1 of mortgage interest may be worth only 15 or 28 cents in tax savings to you. Worse still, experts say, sometimes the interest deductibility will be utterly useless. How and why? Because your mortgage interest deduction and other itemized deductions, combined, may amount to <u>less</u> than the "standard deduction". As a solid evidence of this, it is pointed out that indeed over 70% of all tax filers take the "standard", not the "itemized" deduction, an amount which in 1995 tax year was a sizeable $6,550 for a couple filing jointly.

MYTH #4: That Having A Fixed-Rate Mortgage Protects You From Inflation, Anyway.

As one argument against acceleration, it is contended by some that if you have a fixed-rate mortgage you need not be concerned, anyway, about the cost of interest in that your fixed-rate mortgage shall have protected you against inflation.

Not so at all! What is true is this: that inflation makes buying a home a good investment in comparison to paying rent. What's not true, though, is this: that that, therefore, makes mortgage acceleration a bad or unprofitable idea! From the standpoint of comparing the value of renting versus owning a home, it's generally a fact that one will make out better in terms of inflation by buying rather than renting, since it's generally agreed that as the market value and the demand for homes or apartments increase over the years as a result of inflation, the renter's costs of housing will likely go up as the landlord raises rents to reflect such increase in market value and housing demand. It is agreed that, a buyer who finances a home with a fixed-rate mortgage benefits from inflation in the same way in that for him the housing cost decreases overtime (through the fixed payments and increased buying power) at the same time that the average income will likely grow by at least the same rate of inflation.

---

[*] See, for example, The Wall Street Journal, March 19, 1996.

In order words, in assessing the renting-versus-owning question, the impact of inflation is felt in two ways. And each of them is just as significant and should be equally evaluated. First, the buying power of the dollar is eroded as prices climb (at 2% inflation, it's estimated that $1 today will buy only $0.82 worth of goods in 10 years). Second, the cost of goods rises due to inflation (at 2% increase, an item that costs $1 today will cost $1.22 in 10 years). [See figure 3-1 for the impact of the inflation factor on both the erosion of buying power, and the rise in prices] And when both methods of evaluating the cost of inflation is used, it is found that the renter suffers quite alright due to inflation while the homeowner benefits in that the renter, on the one hand, must pay ever-increasing amounts of housing costs, while, on the other hand, the homeowner enjoys reduced costs over time through fixed payments and increased buying power.

*__Example 1:__ A renter pays $600 per month for an apartment. He had average rent increases that matched inflation at the rate of 2% per year. Ten years later, the same apartment costs him $732 per month.

__Example 2:__ A buyer who has a family monthly income of $3,000 makes mortgage payments of $702 per month, which represents 23.4 percent of the monthly income. Ten years later, the total income—keeping pace with inflation of 2 percent per year—has risen to $3,600. At that point, his housing costs are 19.2 percent of his income.

Clearly, then, there is no question that inflation hurts the renter while it benefits the home-owner; and that buying a home is a good investment in comparison to renting. But here's where

	buying power of one dollar			
year	1%	2%	3%	4%
0	$1.00	$1.00	$1.00	$1.00
5	.95	.90	.86	.82
10	.90	.82	.74	.66
15	.86	.74	.63	.54
20	.82	.67	.54	.44
25	.78	.60	.47	.36
30	.74	.55	.40	.29

	cost per one dollar			
year	1%	2%	3%	4%
0	$1.00	$1.00	$1.00	$1.00
5	1.05	1.10	1.16	1.22
10	1.10	1.22	1.34	1.48
15	1.16	1.35	1.56	1.80
20	1.22	1.49	1.81	2.19
25	1.28	1.64	2.09	2.67
30	1.35	1.81	2.43	3.24

Figure 3-1. Inflation factors for buying power & cost.

---

* These examples are taken, for illustrative purposes here, from Michael C. Thomsett, *Save $ On Your Mortgage: The Mortgage Acceleration Techniques* (John Wiley & Sons), p.25

the myth comes into play: the stated argument, namely, the inflation factor argument, is only a strong one in support of investing in YOUR own home; it is an argument between the renter and the homeowner, not between the homeowner and the lender. It is, in other words, a completely separate issue. Certainly, you gain some financial benefits (call it profits) from being a homeowner relative to having to rent. But after you have secured those benefits, you still come back to the question of the total cost to you: *how fast can you build equity in the property given the total interest costs you'll have to pay the mortgage lender and the proportion of the total profits (it's less) that ultimately go to the HOMEOWNER relative to the lender?*

In sum, mortgage acceleration still makes financial sense even with the fact that you get fixed costs when you buy a home when you consider the actual cost of buying a home versus the reduction in that cost which you can bring about through payment acceleration, and when you consider the fact that interest would still erode (in the lender's favor) those profits you stand to make from renting as opposed to owning. This fact becomes even clearer from a comparison of housing values to interest cost, as in the following example:

*EXAMPLE: If we assume that annual inflation is 2 percent, the total rate of cost per dollar [Fig. 3-1] in 30 years is $1.81. That means that, assuming that the housing values keep pace with inflation, your $100,000 home will be worth $181,000 in 30 years. At the same time, for the $80,000 mortgage you took out on the home at 10 percent interest, (that is, after a 20 percent down payment you shall have made on the house) you will pay $252,742 in interest in 30 years. In other words, your housing costs (what you'll pay and expect to spend on the house) as a homeowner, would have exceeded the rate of inflation (what you expect to get back on the house) by some $71,742. (Note that, using the rate of cost per dollar, Fig. 3-1, you'll find that in order for real estate values to match your housing costs, which is only the break even point, they'll have to rise by more than 3 percent, a rate equal to 150 percent of inflation—quite a daunting feat!)

Hence we see that, even with the protection afforded by a fixed rate of interest, inflation will erode your gains to the point where you may not really have any "net" profit at all.

MYTH #5: *That You Earn More Money Investing Somewhere Else In Something Else*

It's often stated by some financial advisors and investment salespersons that you stand to earn more money by putting the money you invest in making extra mortgage payments in other types of investments. This argument is couched in several ways: that you're better off paying off the home mortgage over the full duration of the mortgage term and thus investing that extra "disposable income" elsewhere; or, that with respect to the equity you accumulate in your home, it's financially foolish and imprudent to leave such huge "idle equity" just sitting in your home and should rather be taken out and be "put to work" in other types of investment; or that building up equity in a home is merely an emblem of poor financial management and that sophisticated financial management calls for you to indulge in "leverage" requiring that you always be in debt to the maximum level you can attain.

---

* Illustration taken from Thomsett, Save $ On Your House Mortgage, p.25.

Such propositions are badly flawed, however. Use of financial leverage (debt or borrowed funds) for investment opportunities which, presumably, may yield better returns, may be a sound financial strategy. But the reality is that leverage is not without cost, it can be an expensive and risky strategy. As one analyst plainly sums its up, "The more you owe, the more you repay, and the longer you will remain in debt."[*] Sure, in given cases it's possible you could exceed, by way of profit, the percentage you pay on your mortgage by investing in some other types of investment. But at what risks? The moment you factor in the risk element into the calculation of yield, and properly compare both the yield and the risk involved, you'll immediately find that there are probably not many other comparable investment options in terms of yield and risk, and that as a general proposition your home is most likely the safest and surest investment available to you.

Consider the issue of the comparative rate of return and the degree of risk for an outside investment relative to mortgage acceleration.

COMPARATIVE RISKS

From the **lender's** standpoint, the risk for him is very minimal, since his mortgage is secured by your home and if you were to fail to meet your mortgage obligations to him he can simply "foreclose" (recover) the property. For the real property **salesperson**, he incurs virtually no risk: he gets paid his commission up front at the time the investment in the property is made.

For **you**, the homebuyer, though, the story is different. It is on YOU that the whole risks lie a hundred percent. Even if we were to accept as guaranteed that you can earn in an outside investment today a better yield than the compound rate you're paying on the mortgage, what's the certainty that you'll be able to earn that yield *every year, year after year for the 30 years or so* your mortgage debt will last? Virtually none! You might be able to be ahead this year, or next. But what about five years hence? Or ten? Or fifteen? It's very doubtful that a string of such favorable yields will continue from any other type of investment over so long a period. The point is that *mortgage investment and accelerated payment of the mortgage are, on the other hand, the one investment that virtually assures such benefits! And mortgage investment is the one investment that has virtually no risk; a home is generally the safest investment available over the long term since money invested in your home has a greater chance of not being spent than money put in any other investments.*

In sum, the point is that you are much less likely to find any other investment that will both yield a higher return <u>and</u> also have a safer risk factor than an investment in a home. The possibility, indeed the probability, is very real that even if you will earn on an outside investment something equal to or better than what you'll get from accelerating on your mortgage, the value of your outside investment could fall, even significantly, over the course of the period. The reality, then, is that if you take the lender's and the salesperson's typical advise of taking out your "idle" home equity funds and "putting it to work" in other types of investment, you will be putting it to work, alright. But for the net benefit of the <u>lender</u> or the <u>salesperson</u>—and not YOURS!

---

[*]   Thomsett, *Save $ On Your Home Mortgage*, p. 109

ILLUSTRATION: Let's see just how unlikely it is that you'll readily be able to find an investment option that will both YIELD a higher return and PROVIDE a safer RISK element than a home investment. Assume a mortgage of $80,000 at 10% interest rate running for a 30-year term, which makes the required payment $702.06 per month for 560 payments.

First, on the yield issue, this would mean that in order to match such a yield, the outside investment you pick would have to yield you 10 percent, compounded monthly, and continue to pay you that yield uninterrupted, year after year for the next 30 years. To see just how much more superior the yield on investment in home mortgage could get relative to the yield from any other investment, let's say that all you do is make a single, one-time-only pre-payment of only $100 towards the mortgage principal in the first month of the 30-year mortgage term. You'll immediately find [See Figures 3-2 and 3-3 below] that the value from that $100 alone is substantial—some $1,984. That one time $100 investment alone is worth so much—as much as taking approximately 3 months off the total term of the loan! Now, if your one-time-only prepayment were to be $1,000, instead of $100, that will be worth (the yield to you) a whopping return of $19,837, and that alone will chop off more than 4 years (28.3 months, exactly) from the total term of the loan! And, because of the peculiar nature of the structure of loan amortization (see the discussion in Section F of Chapter 1), the longer the loan term still remaining on the mortgage (or the larger the rate of interest and/or the balance on the loan), the higher the yield that will accrue to you. (Samples of the yields or payoffs from making varying single, one-time-only pre-payments at the beginning of a mortgage term, are shown in Figure 3-4)

Here's the effect of prepaying $100, one time only, at various interest rates for different terms:

	MORTGAGE INTEREST RATE			
YEARS	**8%**	**10%**	**12%**	**14%**
5	$ 149	$ 165	$ 182	$ 201
10	222	271	330	402
15	331	445	600	307
20	493	733	1,089	1,618
25	734	1,206	1,979	3,245
30	1,094	1,984	3,595	6,508

Figure 3-2. Value of $100 prepayment on $80,000 loan at varying interest rates.

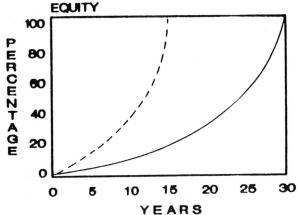

Figure 3-3.

Single payment acceleration, $80,000 loan, 30-year term.
—, scheduled payments; - - -, accelerated payments

Now, the central question is: how does such a yield from investing in home mortgage compare against any other type of investment? For a given alternative investment to match these home-purchase investment yields, that investment in the same amount ($100), must be able to yield 10 percent return, compounded monthly, for no less than the same 30-year term. That is, if you invest $100 or $1,000 today in a stock purchase (assuming that's the investment you choose), it must yield you a return of $1,984 or $19,837, respectively, 30 years from today. In realistic terms, you are plainly unlikely to find such an alternative investment. And, even if you were at all to find one that could, in theory, yield you such a return on a straight line mechanical formula as of today, it will still be unlikely that such investment would be as safe as investing in your home (that the registered high yield of today will continue to be matched for as long as your mortgage term), or that the registered yield of today will still be available (that you would not have spent it) within the next 30-year period—something you would not have to worry about for an investment made in your home.

PAYMENT METHOD	TOTAL PAYMENTS	INTEREST PAYMENTS	AMOUNT SAVED
full amortization, 30 years	$252,735	$172,735	$ —
15-year amortization	154,744	74,744	97,991
add $100 per month	171,937	91,937	80,798
add $200 per month	146,027	66,027	106,708
add $1,000 each year	176,238	96,238	76,497
add $2,000 each year	149,671	69,671	103,064

Figure 3-4 Savings comparison

MYTH #6: That Debt (Mortgage) Acceleration Is Only Good During Times When The Home's Value Is Rising, But Not When It's Falling.

It's a common argument held among many financial professionals and uninformed homeowners alike who are opposed to acceleration, that while mortgage acceleration may be justifiable and proper when the assumption is that a home's value will rise over time, an acceleration plan is unwise when there's a depressed market and the home's value is falling. The argument goes this way, as captured by one analyst.[*] "Paying off your mortgage more rapidly is a smart idea as long as your home's market value is rising. But if your home's value is falling, you're throwing good money after bad."

---

[*] Thomsett, *Save $ On Your Home Mortgage*, p. 153

It's not so, however. In reality, quite to the contrary, this line of reasoning is badly flawed in a few ways. Fundamentally, the flaw in this argument lies in the fact that it assumes the mindset of an investor, not that of a homeowner—that is, it fails to make a distinction between your home as a unique type of long-term investment, and your other investments, a distinction that should be made based not on the paper profits made or potentially to be made (as in the case of other investments, such as stocks or bonds), but on the purpose behind the investment (as in the case of home investment). True, if you make a poor investment in, say, a mutual fund, it may be unwise to continue putting more money into the same fund in a falling stock market. But that will be because, generally when you invest in shares of mutual fund (or similar investments, such as stocks, or the futures), you often do so solely in the hopes of turning a relatively fast profit. And, the moment the profit comes, you take it and then put your money into something else. Not so, though, with real estate investment. With your own home, first of all, the overwhelming part of the appraised value of the object of your investment, the home, is represented by debt, and it may not be that easy for you to simply walk away from a home that has fallen in value when you probably still owe a substantial mortgage debt on it to your lenders. Secondly, with your own home, you are buying a personal asset, personal security, and safety—not a part of a portfolio. You and your family live in the home; you and your family have a place to live. The real, if intangible value and importance of this benefit alone, in and of itself, is immense. In deed, so immense, many home investment and financial analysts contend , that it surpasses the financial value of the home, and of the investment in the home. For, if the homeowner were simply to accept the reality of a depressed market and depreciated value of his home and walk away from the home, what does he and the family do about where to live, or about the money that will be necessary in order to pay for an alternative housing? Furthermore, he and the family will have to face the many other issues that often come with moving: change of job, finding new social contacts, disruption of the continuity of his life and those of his family, finding a new school for the children, etc.

The point, simply, is that because of the unique "personal security" value of owning a home to you, it's not readily practicable for the average homeowner to simply walk away from a house merely because of its falling value, in the same way that he might with respect to other types of investments or assets. And, by the same token, the notion that a homeowner should tie the value of a mortgage acceleration plan to whether the home's value is rising or falling over time, is not the way things work with real estate investment. Rather, with real estate, you'll have to view it as a long-term investment. Given your continuing need for shelter, your home is more than simply an "investment" and the value goes beyond merely its current market value. What all these mean, is that you are all too likely to set your mind on continuing to pay your mortgage debt until it is paid off, regardless of what happens to the home's immediate value. *And hence, since it's to be assumed that you'll probably keep your home for many years even in depressed market, acceleration of your mortgage would still be a sound idea, whether the home's market value rises or falls*, for as it has been demonstrated elsewhere in this manual (see pp. 6 & 21), it's the amount you pay in interest overtime that ultimately determines the true value of your home, and not the momentary rise and fall in its market value.

Finally, look at this argument (i.e., that mortgage acceleration is only good in times of rising home values) this way. Recall the fundamental function and purpose of acceleration of mortgage repayment? It's essentially to reduce your interest expense, isn't it, and, through that, the total cost of your home, and to build your equity more rapidly in the process? The point is that given that, that same acceleration will continue to save you that same interest expense so long as you are an owner of the property, regardless of the home's value. To put it another way, *since acceleration reduces the long-term cost of one's mortgage loan (one's home), it will still make sound financial sense even when the home's market value were to be falling.*

EXAMPLE: Let's say you purchase a home today valued at $120,000 on a 30-year, $100,000 mortgage at 10 percent interest rate. The $120,000 home will cost you a total of $335,925 over the 30-year life of the mortgage. (The $120,000 purchase price plus $215,925 in interest cost on the $100,000 mortgage). You can reduce that cost, however, to $245,410 by acceleration, by repaying the mortgage over, say 19.3 years. You'll save yourself about $90,515. (You'll achieve the same result, by the way, by adding $100 every month to your regular monthly payment of $866.57 to make it $966.57). *Now, if that $120,000 home were to double in value, or stay the same, or falls, it wouldn't make any difference: you still would have had the $215,925 interest expense burden to carry on that property for so long as you own it and haven't yet paid off the mortgage. Hence, in that way and during that time, acceleration (speeding up) of the payments will still continue to save you what it will save you, regardless of the home's value.*

B. Some Potential Vested Interests Of The Mortgage Lenders & Real Estate Salespeople In Propagating The Myths

But why, one might ask, these above-stated myths and 'flawed' arguments, in the first place? What are, at least, some of the possible underlying purposes and motivations for many who champion them?

Michael C. Thomsett, a noted real estate finance expert and author, advances one thesis. While observing that it is the bankers, the mortgage lenders, real estate salespeople, and sellers of investment securities, who generally make the strongest arguments against mortgage repayment acceleration and mortgage pay down, Thomsett adds that "to evaluate an argument, you must always consider the source." Thomsett makes the cogent point that because such persons who argue against mortgage acceleration are often professionals with a vested financial interest who derive their means of livelihood primarily through the generation of commissions or interest from long-term borrowings and investments, such arguments must necessarily be viewed with grave suspicion.

Thomsett sums up in this way, why, in his assessment, it's no surprise that these professionals necessarily take the position they've taken against mortgage acceleration:[*]

> "Lenders benefit when you borrow money or when you pay off a
> loan over the longest possible period. The more acceleration you achieve,
> the lower the lender's total income. Lenders are in the money business,
> meaning they have [to make] loans [to borrowers]. The longer the
> repayments period, the higher the use of that [loan].

---

[*] Thomsett, *Save $ On Your Home Mortgage*, pp.99-100

Salespeople are interested in getting you to borrow money with equity as collateral, because that means more commission income for them. *There is no commission paid on acceleration, so salespeople cannot be expected to objectively compare advantages between investments on which they earn money [long-term loans], and strategies on which they receive nothing [by acceleration of payment]."*

The problem stems primarily from what Thomsett aptly calls the salesperson's "dilemma". The dilemma runs this way. On the one hand, the real estate and mortgage salesperson knows quite well that your investing your money in building up home equity as quickly as possible (i.e., in accelerated repayment of the mortgage) is the more prudent path for you, but on the other hand, he is keenly aware that given the limited cash at your disposal any extra payments you are to put towards accelerated home payments would directly mean less monies that you won't put into investing in his own business which would yield him commission—the stock market, mutual funds, public syndications, or annuities. As Thomsett puts it, the sales person reasons this way: that "if you put in only $2,000 [in investing in things like stocks, bonds and those types of investments he controls, so that you can invest more in accelerating your mortgage payment], the total commission for him is only $160. But if you invest $20,000 [in his type of investments by investing less in acceleration of your mortgage], the commission to him jumps to $1,600."

Consequently, Thomsett explains, the salespersons do the only thing that straightforward business logic and commonsense would dictate that they do: they "appeal to your sense of guilt about how and why you should borrow to the maximum level possible and why you must put your home equity to work...[and how you are] better off paying your mortgage over the full term and investing your 'disposable income' somewhere else."

At the heart of all these, is another fundamental factor, namely, a common mistake often made by the general public. The common misconception and general assumption on the public's part is that investment salespeople (financial planners, advisors, consultants, and the like) necessarily have some special knowledge and expertise that the ordinary person does not have, or that such persons are unaffected by ordinary human bias or self-interest and are almost always objective in their professional advice and in the recommendations they make to clients. In reality, however, such an assumption is not necessarily valid. Indeed, quite the contrary is true. Anyone, for instance, can call himself or herself a financial planner as it requires no particular or specialized knowledge to qualify, and even those having genuine expertise in financial planning invariably acquire such expertise through a background in varied, different disciplines—in life insurance, mutual funds sales, the stock market, and the like. And chances generally are that they don't understand real estate or the real cost of buying a house from the standpoint of the interest costs.

In sum, the point is that any investment advice or general opinions offered by traditional financial planners and investment salespeople on mortgage payment acceleration plans and strategies, should generally be viewed with a critical eye, anyway, and should at least be taken with a grain of salt.

CHAPTER 4
WHY MORTGAGE ACCELERATION WILL GENERALLY BE A SOUND FINANCIAL INVESTMENT FOR THE AVERAGE HOMEOWNER

To be sure, there are many situations, though rarer and fewer in number, when and where mortgage acceleration—i.e., speeding up the pace at which you pay off your mortgage—may not be a smart move to make for a homeowner (see Chapter 5, for example, for an elaboration). By and large, however, it often makes an overwhelming financial sense to do so for the average homeowner. In this chapter, we shall consider some of the major reasons why acceleration is by and large generally a sound financial investment for most homeowners.

Here are the major reasons:

1. Relatively Higher Rate Of Return
By and large, the rate of return you get from your accelerated mortgage payments is higher than the rate you can earn putting the money in most other investments. Here's the point to remember: when you pay ahead on your mortgage, what you're doing is exactly the equivalence of investing; like an ordinary investment, when you make a prepayment on a mortgage, your "return" is the AVOIDANCE OF FUTURE INTEREST, your rate of return on this investment equals the interest rate on the mortgage. In other words, the benefits of (the returns on) a mortgage prepayment is precisely the interest rate of the mortgage as compared to the rate of return available on other investments.

For example, if your mortgage is a high-interest mortgage (say 12 percent), you are actually *losing* that rate of return each month, hence if you were to accelerate that mortgage, say you were to add a dollar to your regular payment, what you actually "earn" on that $1.00 is equally 12 percent—the same as you would earn by placing the same amount in an investment. [See pp. 13-14 for a fuller discussion of this].

2. Funds Invested Through Acceleration Are Extremely Safe
Judged not merely in terms of the percentage YIELD (the rate of return) you're paying on your mortgage relative to a different kind of investment, but in terms of the comparable RISK level as well, chances are that you'll find that by and large your home is most likely the safest investment available for you. With respect to your home, for example, through your homeowner's insurance, your home is secured from most hazards and risks; because of your maintenance of the house and personal involvement with it, and because of your improvements on the property and based on historical information, you have every reason to believe that your home will grow steadily in value over the years. But how, on the other hand, does this compare with the average

other investment? *An investment, such as a mutual fund, for example, may have the same historical YIELD as your house. But even if it does, it will hardly match up in terms of the RISK level: it is not insured, its growth rate is neither assured nor reasonably predictable, and the same is true with respect to the value of the shares over a long-term period.* [See pp. 26-28 for a fuller discussion of this]

3. With Acceleration You Can Cut The Cost Of Your Home & Reduce The Repayment Period Dramatically

Looked at from any number of ways, the reduction in the real total cost of your house that results directly from mortgage acceleration could be very dramatic indeed. Examine the amortization tables in Appendix A. Do you see how rapidly the repayment term falls—just by paying a few dollars extra per month!? Simply paying $100 *additional* every month, for example, on an $80,000, 30-year, fixed-rate mortgage at 10 percent interest rate, will drastically reduce the payment term by about 12 years, and reduce your cost by more than $80,000. By paying off your mortgage over a 15 year period rather a than 30 year period [on an $80,000, 10 percent mortgage], you will reduce the cost of your home by as much as $100,000. [See pp. 2 & 9 for a fuller discussion of this].

4. Mortgage Acceleration Enables You To Better Plan Your Financial Future

As has been emphasized over and over again in various sections of this manual, mortgage acceleration is the one investment that cuts costs and repayment term in a home most quickly. By making it possible for you to own your own home free and clear many, many years sooner, one direct benefit of mortgage acceleration, is to squarely put you in charge of your financial future.

Let's say, for example, that you repay your mortgage in 15 years instead of 30 years. What that means for you, is that the burden on your family's budget shall have been relieved that much sooner, making it that much easier for you to enjoy greater financial freedom in your budget and greater freedom to meet other family expenses of the future. A rapid build up of equity from acceleration means greater secured borrowing power; as your equity increases so will your ability to finance improvements in the house to refinance the mortgage or borrow money in the future. You will, for example, be better able to borrow additional money, say for a swimming pool or for a garage, to your home, if need be.

It is the common conclusion by most credible personal financial experts and professional planners, that because mortgages almost always represent the largest single debt for most people and families, speeding up your mortgage debt repayment and paying it off as fast as possible, or you can afford to, is the essential key to getting out of the dreaded American mortgage 'debt trap' and for getting on the path to financial redemption. David Grank, noted author of long-time best selling *Godly Finances:The Bible Way To Pay Off Your Home, puts* it this way: "One vital key to getting out of debt is paying off your home mortgage ahead of schedule."

5. Mortgage Acceleration Increases The Homeowner's Equity

One important feature and advantage of mortgage acceleration, often either not quite understood or stubbornly ignored by critics, is the "forced" element of acceleration—the fact that since mortgage payment is an illiquid investment which one cannot readily get back once it is spent, the homeowner is forced to build equity in the home over a relatively long period of time even where ordinarily he probably might not have had the personal discipline or disposition to do so.

Indeed, so strong is this advantage held by mortgage acceleration, that contrary to the conventional thinking that this advantage generally makes sense mostly if one plans to stay in one's home for the full mortgage term, acceleration is frequently as sensible and helpful both when you plan either to move within a short time, or to stay on indefinitely. In either case, the more you accelerate *today*, the more rapidly you'll be able to build equity in your home within a few years. In either case, your family will have greater financial security based on the degree of equity you shall have built up in your home in that the sooner you are able to cut down the mortgage debt, or to eliminate it, the less risk you carry vis-à-vis the lender.

6. Mortgage Acceleration Provides You Financial & Budget Flexibility

Probably one of the most attractive and useful features of mortgage acceleration, is its flexibility and voluntarity; you can start, stop, increase, or decrease the degree of your investment whenever and however you desire. This is a great advantage for most people as it fits in perfectly with the limitations of a personal budget. You might have agreed to a long-term, 30-year mortgage, just to qualify for the lender's requirements for a loan at the time of your loan application, but still retain the option to repay the mortgage more rapidly if you happen to find yourself with more abundant resources in the future. With acceleration, you're in control. It's both flexible and voluntary: you decide if and when you wish to make additional payments, you decide in what amounts the additional payments are to be made, and you can start and stop the payment plan at any time you want, and increase or decrease the payments as and when you want.

This flexibility to alter your investment, sharply contrasts, on the other hand, with the lack of flexibility you'll get if you were to start out with a short-term mortgage with practically little or no room for making an acceleration of the payments. Here, in a short-term mortgage, say a 15-year term, you lack *choice* of paying off the loan more rapidly; the only realistic option you have, is to make your regular monthly payment every month [see pp. 46 & 72 for more on this issue}.

CHAPTER 5
SOME FEW SITUATIONS WHEN IT MAY NOT MAKE GOOD FINANCIAL SENSE TO ACCELERATE YOUR MORTGAGE PAYMENTS

In various sections of this manual (see, for example, Chapters 3 & 4) we have dwelt on the many various profound advantages of mortgage acceleration to the homeowner, firmly holding to the position that by and large acceleration is a sound financial strategy for the average homeowner. Elsewhere, we have detailed many of the myths and flawed arguments often advanced by the few among the financial professionals who argue against acceleration. (See Chapter 3).

In this chapter, we explain, in a more elaborate and specific term, the instances and situations, though far fewer in number, when it may, nevertheless, be an insensible and illadvised idea to undertake an acceleration program.

Those Situations When Acceleration May Not Be A Sensible Idea

As might be expected, mortgage acceleration, not unlike everything else in life, is not perfect; it may perfectly make sense most of the time, but certainly not all the time. Such situations, when acceleration may not be smart or advisable, are few and far between, however.

Here are such circumstances when it may be ill-advised or a poor idea to proceed with an acceleration program:

1. When You Can, In Fact, Earn A Higher Return Investing Elsewhere
In theory, if you would find another investment that could, in reality, yield you a rate of return that is the same as, or higher than, the compounded rate of interest you pay on your mortgage, and which has a comparable level of risk, then you may be better off not paying off your mortgage rapidly, and putting the extra payments, rather, in that other type of investment. But, as we have attempted to show elsewhere in the manual (see Myth #5, at p. 25, for example), the real problem is this: would you often find such other investments having such potentials in terms of giving you a better yield, as well as better level of risk?

The point is that for a proper and complete comparison, the exercise must include, as well, two other elements: the risk factor and availability of cash. For example, money put into, say, corporate stock, does contain greater risks than money put into accelerating a mortgage. And, secondly, money put into such investment is very liquid, making it a real possibility that such investment could be taken out and spent at any time in the course of the (30 year) comparative period. When such risk factor and availability problems are assessed and factored in and placed against the comparative yields for other types of investment, you'll often find that it's generally difficult to find an outside investment which matches up against a mortgage investment. [see p. 26]

2. When You Can't Afford It

A very important circumstance, often very real in many homeowners' lives and experience, when it would be highly ill-advised and not a good idea to undertake an acceleration of the mortgage payments, is when your budget is already so tight and restricted that you can barely afford, already, your existing regular monthly payments. It would not be financially sensible to attempt to speed up paying off your mortgage if it leaves your savings and investment pool so depleted that you or the family might suffer grave inconvenience and hardship if the roof were to leak or your car were to need a new tire. Furthermore, if you will have to borrow to meet anticipated large expenditures ahead, such as for a child's college tuition, or a new car, such would be a perfect situation when and where it will be counter-productive to attempt paying off the mortgage more speedily given that you'll probably pay more in interest for the extra borrowed funds than on your mortgage. For example, evidently it will make absolutely no financial sense for you to pay off, say, a 9 percent mortgage while continuing to carry a big balance on credit card debts you ran up which charge you 18, 19 or 20 percent interest additionally, especially since it's now a fact that credit card interest is no longer tax-deductible.

In short, only when you have made certain that putting in that ***additional*** mortgage payment won't leave you too strapped -- and that you have established a reasonable reserve fund for extreme emergencies, as elaborated in Chapter 2 and Section 3 below—should you move on with an accelerated payment program on your mortgage. To put it another way, *this is to say that it's conceivable, even probable, that your present budget at the time of the start of the mortgage term may not allow for an acceleration. If so, there will be nothing wrong with you waiting. At the proper time in the future when you find yourself able to achieve budget sufficiency, say, from eliminating some expenses or from earning a higher monthly income, you may then commence an acceleration plan—properly and prudently.*

3. When You Have Not, or Cannot Afford to, Set Up a Reserve

In Chapter 2, the case is made, quite emphatically, that an emergency reserve fund must always be FIRST established before a mortgage prepayment (acceleration) program should be undertaken, as it is stressed that for many it may be more practicable to design a reasonable "balanced" program that sensibly marries together a reserve fund and an accelerated payment plan in such a way as to achieve the double objectives of creating a highly liquid and safe emergency cushion, while at the same time applying reasonable amount of money towards equity build-up and interest cost reduction in your home. Here, we reiterate that one circumstance where it will be highly fraught with risks and therefore ill-advised to embark on a mortgage acceleration program, would be where you have not put away a reserve fund with which to meet any near-term potential emergencies of the future prior to the acceleration program. [See Chapter 2 for a more elaborate treatment of the higher priority of establishing an emergency reserve fund before acceleration.]

CHAPTER 6
ACCELERATION PLANS FOR ADJUSTABLE RATE MORTGAGES

A. What Is An Adjustable-Rate Mortgage?

An "Adjustable Rate" type of Mortgage (ARM) is more fully defined and explained in Appendix A. For our immediate purposes as a background material, however, suffice it to say simply that an ARM type of mortgage is basically a mortgage with no fixed rate of interest; one for which, instead, the rate of interest attached to it fluctuates upwards and downwards in tandem with one of the established cost-of-money indices, such as the "prime rate", the rate banks charge their most credit worthy customers for money lent them. In an ARM type of loan contract, the lender has the right to increase the annual interest rate chargeable for the mortgage loan as the cost of money to the lender increases. That is, by agreement the degree to which the lender can increase the interest rate you'll pay is tied to an agreed-upon outside index that measures interest rates. Frequently the mortgage contract will call for the lender to place a "cap" in the form of interest rate or the amount of mortgage payment, or a combination thereof, on the extent of the fluctuation allowable from one period of adjustment to the next. Hence, as the agreed outside index rate rises (if and when it does), your lender will usually increase your loan rate to the same degree (up to the level of the agreed maximum or "cap").

Adjustable Rate Mortgages (ARMS) go by a variety of other names, such as: "rollover" mortgages, "flexible rate," and "variable rate" mortgages.

Until the late 1970s, adjustable-rate mortgages were virtually unheard of. Before then, the standard mortgage in the real estate industry had been the traditional 30-year fixed rate term mortgage. But then, starting from the late 1970s and especially in the early 1980s, lenders found it necessary to create for their own benefits the adjustable-rate type of mortgage. Why? Because as the severe inflationary conditions in the country at the time had driven interest rates sky high (it was as high as 20 percent and more at one time), mortgage lenders suddenly found themselves confronted with one critical problem: the fixed interest, long term mortgage loans they had given out to homeowners were yielding them less and less income than the existing cost of money for the lenders. As the interest rates rose the banks and mortgage lenders had, for example, to pay increasingly higher rates on customer deposits to attract and keep their depositors. But the income for these lenders – the interest they received on mortgage loans – was absolutely flat since the mortgage had been issued months and years before at "fixed" rates. The result was massive losses on the part of the mortgage lender. Indeed, so severe was the impact of this phenomenon upon the lenders that many of the major mortgage lending institutions of the period, principally the savings and loan associations or S & Ls, had gone bankrupt, while others barely survived.

The response of the mortgage bankers and lenders was to create a new type of mortgages—the adjustable-rate mortgages. The idea was to ensure that in the event that inflation sets in and the interest rates sky rocket, the homeowner would pay more on their mortgages and thus the lender is guaranteed that his income would always rise as well.

B. Can You Prepay An Adjustable Rate Mortgage?

An important primary question for this chapter, is: can an adjustable mortgage be prepaid as one would any conventional fixed mortgage? And, if so, how do you do it, what types of prepayment plans can apply to the ARM types?

The answer to the first question is YES. You certainly can prepay your adjustable rate type of mortgage as well, just as you can do with any other conventional mortgage. In the case of an adjustable or variable rate mortgage, acceleration (i.e., prepayment) of the loan principal might just involve a little more complicated bookkeeping. The big difference is that for an adjustable rate mortgage, every time the interest rate on your mortgage payments change, the mortgage amortization schedule you'd have to follow will have to change too. To be able to assess the actual amount of principal due on the next payment, you'll virtually need to obtain a new mortgage amortization schedule virtually every time there's an adjustment in your mortgage, a feat which will be virtually impossible except to a person with access to computer with the proper software to produce your amortization schedule with each change.

What this means, therefore, is that with adjustable-rate mortgages, a different strategy of acceleration is required. With an adjustable or variable rate type of mortgage, not only are you interested in reducing the years and total interest cost; you must also plan ahead of increases in the interest rate, and, thirdly, you must at the same time make sure that the acceleration plan you adopt is practicable in terms of fitting within your monthly budget.

C. Adjustable-Rate Mortgage Acceleration (Prepayment) Plans

There are two ways *by which to approach an acceleration program with respect to an adjustable-rate mortgage:*

1. Make an acceleration plan having a higher monthly payment than required and which will remain level throughout the loan term.

2. Offset interest rate increases with a correspondingly high monthly payment.

---

* The exposition in this section is largely adapted from Michael C. Thomsett's *"Save $ On Your House Mortgage"* (John Wiley & Sons) pp. 76-85, to whom the present author is greatly indebted.

Assumptions:

For the purposes of this analysis, assume the following about the loan:

1. That the original loan, an adjustable-rate one, is for $80,000.

2. That the interest loan starts at 8 percent, and the lender is entitled to increase it by no more than 1 percent per year.

3. That the loan has a lifetime cap of 5 points, meaning that the maximum the interest rate can rise to is 13 percent (8 + 5).

4. That the lender will apply the maximum allowable increases each year. (Experts caution that this is always a fair assumption to make with an adjustable-rate mortgage; chances are, it is said, that your interest rate will rise at the maximum speed allowed by the contract and will then remain at that level for the balance of the term.)

Using the above assumptions about changing interest rates, the minimum required monthly payments for 15-year and 30-year terms are as follows, as shown in Figure 6-1

YEARS	INTEREST RATE	MONTHLY PAYMENT	
		15-YEAR	30-YEAR
1	8%	$ 764.53	$ 587.02
2	9	811.42	643.70
3	10	859.69	702.06
4	11	909.28	761.86
5	12	960.14	822.90
6-end	13	1,012.20	884.96

Figure 6-1. Monthly cost of $80,000 adjustable-rate loan (at 8% with 5-point cap).

Plan #1: Pay At Higher But Level Rate

This plan calls for you to pay more than you are required every month, based on the interest rate, but to pay *the same amount* every month. For example, in the case of a 30-year loan of $80,000, the required payment starts out, at the 8 percent rate, at $587.02 per month. The interest rate, under our assumptions, is expected to increase by 1 percent each year, and the maximum that the interest can rise to is 13 percent – attainable by the 6th year. So, what you seek to do would be to establish your monthly payments at about the same amount required to pay off the loan if it had a fixed rate of 13 percent (the maximum under the terms of the loan) – meaning, $885 per month.

If you were to fix the payments at $885 per month, the entire loan will be paid off in about 16 years, instead of 30 years, and it will save you more than $137,000 in interest. Figure 6-2 below shows what happens if payments of $885 are made every month.

YEAR	INTEREST RATE	PAYMENT REQUIRED	PAYMENT MADE
1	8%	$587.02	$885.00
2	9	643.70	885.00
3	10	702.06	885.00
4	11	761.86	885.00
5	12	822.90	885.00
6–end	13	884.96	885.00

Figure 6–2 Plan 1: level payments, $80,000 loan, 30-year term

Here's what a summary of the amortization rate at the adjusted increasing rates during the first 5 years, will look like:

End of Year	Rate	Interest Paid	Principal Paid	Balance
				$80,000.00
1	8%	$6,241.76	$4,378.24	75,621.76
2	9	6,756.02	3,863.98	71,757.78
3	10	7,013.42	3,606.58	68,151.20
4	11	7,334.25	3,285.75	64,865.45
5	12	7,622.21	2,997.79	61,867.66

From this point forward, from the 6th year, the interest rate will be fixed at 13 percent. But you'll continue the payments at $885 per month, and the loan will be paid off in another 11 years.

The important point to note with this example, is that all the acceleration action takes place *during the first 5 years* – but the benefits of that acceleration is to take 14 years off the total repayment period. The amount that goes towards paying the principal during these early years declines each year due to the rising interest rates. Then, when the maximum rate has been reached, the yearly principal portion will begin to increase. At that point the loan balance will decline in the same manner as a fixed-rate mortgage does.

The advantage of this method is that you have the opportunity of paying down the loan at an initially higher rate than required under your contract. A drawback of the method, however, is that the monthly payment it requires might just be beyond your budget. The important point to note is this: for this plan to work, you must be sure that you can afford to pay the higher amounts <u>now</u>. For example, a central assumption in the above example without which the plan could not work, is that the homeowner can afford to pay the required $885 each month, or some $300 more per month than the required initial monthly payment.

Plan #2: Pay At Slightly Higher Rate & Adjust it Each Year
Let's assume that you can't afford to make the level of higher payments called for under Plan #1 above, and that the $885 is too high for your current budget. What other option is open to you? You can go for an acceleration plan that will be more practical and affordable: just pay the mortgage at a rate slightly above the required initial amount, adjust it each year, as the interest rate increases.

For example, under the assumptions made above, the interest rate will increase by 1 percent per year. To accelerate under this Plan #2, you can simply pay at a rate that is 1 percent above what's required. Thus, if a mortgage contract starts out at 8 percent per year, all you do is pay the amount that would be required at 9 percent. If the rate is raised at the end of the year to 9 percent, you increase your payment to the 10 percent level, and so on.

On the $80,000 30-year loan, the 1 percent jump will make a difference of $60 per month. This plan, with its acceleration of payments at a constantly higher rate than is required, has the effect of equalizing both the yearly interest expense and the payments to principal.

Here's what a summary of the plan looks like as in Figure 6-3.

YEAR	INTEREST RATE	PAYMENT REQUIRED	PAYMENT MADE
1	8%	$587.02	$643.70
2	9	643.70	702.06
3	10	702.06	761.86
4	11	761.86	822.90
5	12	822.90	884.96
6-end	13	884.96	936.31

Figure 6–3 Plan 2: principal offset, $80,000 loan, 30-year term

As could be seen from Fig. 6-3, from the point you reach the maximum rate of 13 percent (the maximum under the terms of the loan), you equalize the monthly payments at $936.31 per month,

Here's what a summary of the amortization rate during the first 5 years will look like under this plan:

End of Year	Rate	Interest Paid	Principal Paid	Balance
				$80,000.00
1	8%	$6,350.56	$1,373.84	78,626.16
2	9	7,019.31	1,405.41	77,220.75
3	10	7,655.19	1,487.13	75,733.62
4	11	8,250.41	1,624.39	74,109.23
5	12	8,794.89	1,824.63	72,284.60

From the first payment in the 6th year, the payment is increased to $936.31 per month and fixed at that amount till the end. Under this plan, by simply staying 1 percent point ahead of the annual interest rate, the result will be a repayment schedule of approximately 19 years, cutting 11 years off your mortgage term and netting you a savings of more than $100,000 on the overall cost of your home. This method also enables you to increase the amount going to your principal (equity build up) each year, as it offsets the rise in interest costs.

The prime advantage of this method over the first method, is that under it the rate of loan amortization is more *controlled* and *gradual* hence your monthly payment increases gradually. It does not impose too high a rate of acceleration; rather, its aim is to match rising interest over several years. Consequently, this acceleration method is probably more realistic, more likely to suit the average homeowner's budget in that your mortgage payments would presumably be steadily rising in tandem with the rise in your income over the years. On the other hand, given that it does not impose too high a rate of acceleration, it will not save as much interest as Plan #1, [for example, Plan #1 reduces $33,000 more than Plan #2, and total repayment occurs 3 years sooner], but for most people it is the practical method.

Primarily designed to match rising interest over the years, here's the amount of each year's mortgage payment increase over the required payment level:

Year	Payment	Amount of Increase	Percent of Increase
1	$643.70	$56.68	9.7%
2	702.06	58.36	9.1
3	761.86	59.80	8.5
4	822.90	61.04	8.0
5	884.96	62.06	7.5
6	936.31	51.35	5.8

Notice that, to be sure, the amount of each year's increased payment is slightly higher than the year before (up until the first 5 years), but that the percentage of increase declines over the same time – meaning that as long as your income can rise through the years of your home ownership, you should be steadily able to afford the increases in the mortgage payments.

The good news is that, as with virtually all acceleration plans, either one of the two acceleration plans in our example will reduce the total cost of your home, substantially, by more than $100,000 over the life of the mortgage. Here is how full amortization compares under the two prepayment plans:

	30-YEAR TERM	PLAN 1	PLAN 2
total payments	$307,698	$169,920	$203,086
less: original loan	80,000	80,000	80,000
interest expense	$227,698	$ 89,920	$123,086
years	30	16	19
amount saved		$137,778	$104,612

Figure 6–4 Accelerating with an adjustable rate

CHAPTER 7
OVERCOMING THE INHERENT 'DILEMMA' THAT'S INVOLVED IN DOING PAYMENT ACCELERATION: BEING ABLE TO AFFORD THE EXTRA PAYMENTS IT REQUIRES

A.   The Homeowner's Payment Acceleration 'Dilemma'

In the preceding chapters of the manual (see, especially Chapter 4), it has been pretty much established that by and large acceleration (speeding up) of mortgage payment makes a great deal of financial sense for the average homeowner, and that it affords the homeowner incredible financial savings in the total cost of his or her home ownership. In the same vein, the point is well established, as well, that because of the systemic swing which occurs in the amortization structure of mortgages from *high interest* payments in the EARLY YEARS, to higher payments of the *principal* during the LATER YEARS, mortgage acceleration, or prepayment of the mortgage, has this profound implication for the average homeowner: *the sooner the homeowner can begin a mortgage acceleration program and make additional extra payments towards his mortgage, the lower his ultimate OVERALL cost for the home's ownership, and the more dramatic is the financial difference it makes for him.*

The generally acknowledged financial benefits and advantages of a timely program of mortgage payment acceleration to the average homeowner is all well and good. *In the final analysis, however, when it comes down to the practical matter of actually undertaking a payment acceleration program, there is, nevertheless, often a harsh reality that many, many homeowners frequently have to confront. It is the harsh reality of what has been characterized as the homeowner's prepayment "dilemma": namely, that for most home buyers or owners the problem is that they simply can't afford to put any extra or additional money into their mortgage payment.* Indeed, a primarily question for the average homeowner, especially one buying his or her first house, is clearly the affordability of a mortgage acceleration program – can he or she afford a prepayment (payment of extra or additional amount) in the first place? The dilemma is frequently very real. On the one hand, given all the great financial advantages inherent in mortgage acceleration, the average homeowner would all too likely love to be able to begin an accelerated mortgage payment almost immediately so as to build up equity and own his (her) property free and clear as speedily as possible. On the other hand, however, the reality is that he may be lacking the income to be able to afford making the larger or additional payments that an accelerated payment would call for and still be able to qualify for the mortgage loan. An acceleration payment program realistically means having to make HIGHER payments, and in realistic terms that may often be beyond the budget of many home buyers or owners to undertake at a given point in time. Indeed, a common reality for many home buyers is that they can barely afford the long-term payment plan (usually the 30-year term) even as it is, even with two working spouses, and any <u>additional</u> payments for them on top of that may be difficult, if not impossible.

In fact, this issue may be even more fundamental than that. If you are like the overwhelming majority of home buyers (and owners) in America, chances are that the affordability or ability-to-pay factor – and how it relates initially to your being able to qualify for a loan at the time of your mortgage application – might have been the primary reason why you had to take on the longer term, 30-year or so mortgage you now have, in the first place. In fact, the odds are probably high that at the time you were initially applying for your present mortgage you probably had some fairly good idea, even if vaguely, that you would probably be better off with a shorter-term kind of mortgage than a longer-term one, and if it had been all up to you, you might have likely opted for a shorter-term mortgage, say a 15 or 20 year one. A 15 or 20-year mortgage for you would have meant that your house would cost you less, but your monthly payments would have been much higher, and you probably were very much aware of that. But, you probably were aware, as well, that if your lender were to have applied the typical 4 to 1 ratio formula between your income at the time and your required monthly payments, you might not have qualified for the shorter-term 15 or 20-year loan. And that's probably why you had to take the longer-term mortgage just so you could hold down the monthly payments and get the lender's approval for your loan application!

As one respected mortgage expert aptly observed, "Given the big extra interest burden [involved in a longer term mortgage, relative to a shorter term one], why the popularity of 30-year loans [among home buyers]? It comes down to the affordability of the monthly payments. It's quite possible that the difference between having to pay $877.57 a month [on a 30-year; $100,000 loan at 10% interest] and $1,074.61a month [for a 15-year term on the same loan] is the difference between being able to afford a home or not."[*] He added: "Nevertheless, the basic principle here is that consumers should take the shorter-term loan if they can manage the monthly payments."

The point is that it's no secret that for most people, the strain on their budget is a major, if not the dominant consideration why they take out a longer-term, 30 year or so mortgage, in the first place, as opposed to a shorter term one; that were it that their personal budget could permit a higher (i.e., additional) mortgage payment per month at the time they had applied for the loan, they probably might have opted for a shorter-term mortgage plan, in the first place, which would have meant that for them, they would have already been engaged, more or less, in the practice of MORTGAGE ACCELERATION from the very beginning. *To put it another way, what we are saying is that generally speaking, the average homebuyer and owner fundamentally desires and wants an "accelerated" payment of his mortgage. He's generally aware, even if vaguely, that people come out ahead financially by taking the shorter-term loan; and, like most people, he very much likes the psychological feeling of having the loan paid off quicker and owning his home free and clear. But, typically, though he would have preferred a shorter-term mortgage plan, he has to take on the longer-term loan initially, primarily because he had to deal with the immediate problem of the moment at the time of his purchase of the house: being able to qualify*

---

[*] John R. Dorfman, *The Mortgage Book*, p.71

initially for a loan with the lender. * In sum, if given the choice, in terms of being able to afford it—and assuming he knows he not only can, but should do so, which most of them seemingly do – the average home buyer would generally prefer to have a shorter, faster (i.e., accelerated) payment of his mortgage, anyway, and to start off on the process at the earliest time possible. The downside of this initial choice by the homeowner to pick a longer-term mortgage, however, is that that very choice comes with a very high price tag for him: it stretches out his mortgage payments over an extended, longer period of years though lowering his monthly payments; but most significantly, it means for him that he'll pay far, far more in total interest expense, and that he'll take much longer time to pay off the mortgage debt burden.

Such is the nature of the average homeowner's financial 'dilemma' in being able to undertake an acceleration of his mortgage repayment!

B. The Practical Solution to the Dilemma

Given the above described reality for the average home buyer, is there any way then by which you, the homeowner or intending home buyer, will be able conveniently to afford prepaying or accelerating your mortgage? A legitimate question to ask, would be if you were apparently not able to afford making a higher mortgage payment some years or so ago at the time you purchased your home, how is it then that you can now necessarily afford to do so today?

The answer is that there is a fundamental difference: with a properly planned acceleration program, such as is being proposed or recommended in this manual, you have complete control and flexibility which you do not have with your mortgage amortization obligations as laid down for you by your lenders. There are no restrictions against prepayments or early payment of the principal. You can start early payments of the principal at any time, and you can make the extra payments in any amounts. True, the earlier you start out on such payments, the better for you and the greater the benefit you'll derive. But what you can have with an acceleration program is a PRACTICAL program – one that you can tailor to fit within the particular limitations of your family budget. No more do you have to be restricted to the repayment terms set by the lender; rather, this time, you can create your own plan based on what you know you can handle.

What is to be emphasized, is that because there is great flexibility with mortgage acceleration, there is, actually, an advantage later down the road for you, in first taking out at the time of the home purchase a longer-term mortgage (say, a 25 or 30-year one), in terms of what you could afford to maintain at the time with your then existing income. On the one hand, it's within your rights and you can simply stay with the 25 or 30-year term mortgage and pay off the loan according to the long-term "amortization" requirements of the mortgage contract. Or, you can, on the other hand, opt to pay the 30-year term mortgage but at speedied-up rate that will retire the debt sooner, say in a 15-year period – if, at some point along the way, you now find that you can afford to make *extra* payments. And, still, if at some point along the way you again find that you cannot now afford the extra payments, you can again revert to the lower monthly required payments whenever you want. And this can go on, back and forth. Thus, by initially agreeing to

---

* Typically, lenders evaluate the risk of granting a mortgage loan based on the applicant's current income at the time of the application and his apparent ability to make the monthly payments. For a mortgage payment of $702 per month, for example (on a 30-year, 10% $80,000 loan), the lender might typically require the applicant to earn <u>four</u> times that amount per month, meaning $2,800. But for a 15-year term, for the same amount the required monthly payment you would have to pay would be $860, which would mean that you would have to be earning at least $3,440 per month for you to qualify for the same loan amount.

a 30-year repayment term but then having the option and flexibility to repay the loan sooner, if and when you want to or find that you can afford it, you would be taking control of your financial future with regard to your mortgage.

In fact, according to mortgage financing experts, even when you can readily afford it and have the minimum income that's required for one to qualify with the lender for a higher monthly payment, it still isn't always smart or necessarily advisable that you start out committing yourself to a shorter payment term with HIGHER payments. Rather, experts say, a better strategy could be to commit initially to a longer-term mortgage, to say a 30-year as opposed to 15-year term, and then be prepared to accelerate the repayment according to how the family budget permits, or the income conditions allow, in the future. This way, they contend, you'll retain the critical element of the flexibility to go in one direction, or the other, as your financial circumstances may warrant – either to stick to the contracted 30-year payment schedule, if you cannot afford to make any extra payments beyond that, or to make extra payments and retire the debt sooner, if some where along the way you find you can afford it.

Thus, under your own self-designed mortgage repayment plan, it's up to you and what you decide, for example, whether or when you should accelerate your repayment; it's up to you to decide by how much you may accelerate your payment at any given time based on your current budget and the changes in your financial circumstances (the addition of another child in the family, higher property taxes or insurance cost, raises in earnings from employment, new and higher (or lower) paying job, loss of employment, illness, maternity leave, etc.), and it's up to you to decide how soon or how slowly you wish to retire your mortgage debt and own your home free and clear. You might decide in the fifth year of your 30-year mortgage, for example, that you can afford then to put in an extra $25 per month to your regular monthly payment, or $50, $60, or whatever. You could decide to completely eliminate the accelerated payment after staying with an increased payment plan for one month, or one year, or whatever the amount of time you choose, due to the personal financial circumstances in your life and your budget situation. You could increase the rate of acceleration as your family income increases, or you could reduce it as it decreases. And so on and so forth. *The point is that because of the great flexibility of the accelerated payment program, its potential for use by a homeowner in devising a beneficial payment plan is infinitely varied and unlimited.*

On the other hand, imagine what would have been your condition if what you had were the shorter, rather than the longer-term mortgage, to work with? Suppose, for example, you were to have started out having, not a 30-year mortgage term, but a 15-year term whereby you contracted to make relatively higher payments every month? In such a situation your choices would have been rigidly fixed to only one option and you will not have the flexibility you might just need in the future to adjust your payment level to suit your changing financial needs, resources or circumstances.

In sum, in general it will often be wiser to start off with a longer term mortgage that you can comfortable pay at the time of your loan commitment, and then try to devise a personal repayment term that can change with the financial means and changes in your life—precisely as you would with a mortgage prepayment or accelerated payment program.

EXAMPLE: Let's say you have your own self-devised payment plan based on an existing mortgage for $80,000 with a 30-year term at 10 percent interest, which had originally called for monthly payments of $702.06 for 360 months, but that immediately after you signed the contract you commenced making payments in the higher amounts of $859.69 ($157.63 additional), anyway, with the aim of liquidating the loan in just 15 years. [See Figure 7-1 below] Then, 5 years into the mortgage, you have gotten a new job with lower pay and you find you're having difficulties making the higher payments.

Because you had initially committed to a longer repayment term, you have a pleasant advantage in that you are in a position to be flexible in what size of monthly payments you may make – so long as you do not go below the minimum required payment. Hence, at this point, you can completely eliminate the additional payments and revert to the required minimum payment of $702.06, or if you find your new income can still allow you to pay something extra, say $50, above the minimum but not anything quite as much as the $157.63 extra you have previously been paying, then you can simply reduce the additional payments you make to only $50 per month. You can continue to make that lower extra payment for an indefinite length of time, and if your financial circumstances should change again in the future, you can adjust your payments again and again, downwards or upwards, to conform to what you can afford.

Years	Payment	Years	Payment
15	$859.69	23	$741.74
16	836.72	24	733.91
17	816.97	25	726.96
18	799.87	26	720.78
19	785.01	27	715.28
20	772.02	28	710.37
21	760.62	29	705.98
22	750.60	30	702.06

Figure 7-1. **Monthly payment required on an $80,000 loan (30 years at 10% interest) for Different Pay-off Dates Selected.**

CHAPTER 8
SOME DIFFERENT TYPES OF PRE-PAYMENT PLANS AVAILABLE. CHOOSING AN APPROPRIATE ONE FOR YOU.

A. The Basic Essentials Of A Workable Pre-Payment Plan

In previous chapters of the manual (see Chapters 2, 5 & 7), the point is amply made that though mortgage acceleration (mortgage pre-payment) should ideally be implemented as quickly as possible as it will more drastically reduce the overall cost of the home purchase that much sooner, the most important consideration and constraint in determining how, when, or even whether to commence a specific type of pre-payment program, and in what amounts, is, ultimately, what your budget can bear. There are, of course, different types of pre-payment plans you can choose from. The central point to be made about this, however, is simply this: *whatever type of pre-payment plan or program you adopt, if it is to be successful and workable in the end, it must be realistic, practical, and financially affordable to you in terms of your own budget. A realistic mortgage acceleration (pre-payment) plan must also be and remain flexible, able to adapt and operate within the context of the ever-shifting limitations of your financial resources and personal budget.*

In this chapter, we show some five different types of acceleration plans or methods by which you can speed up the repayment of your mortgage debt, and offer some explanations of their respective advantages. Each plan works in essentially similar fashion and brings about dramatic savings to the homeowner. On your own part as a homeowner, you are free to choose any one of the plans, or even a combination of several plans – within the context of what is most suited to your budget and personal financial goals, what your priorities are, and your current financial status. The plan (or plans) you choose must, however, be practical (given the particular limitations of income and the other expenses you have to meet). It is also very important that the plan you choose be one that you will be able to stick to and systematize, and that it be one that you will be able to work into your weekly or monthly routine. For example, choosing a prepayment plan that has a specific amount, and paying that amount each month – as in a Fixed Term Pre-Payment Plan, for example – could be deemed an attractive plan by a particular homeowner because of its extreme simplicity and because it makes for a consistent plan. With such a plan you are less likely to miss the extra money you pay, for example, as the payments will readily become an integral part of your budget.

B. The Five Different Types of Pre-payment Plans We'll Consider

The five types of pre-payment plans we'll discuss here are the following:

    1.   Flat or Fixed-Sum Pre-payment Plan
    2.   Principal-only (Variable-Sum) Pre-payment Method
    3.   Fixed Term Pre-payment Plan or Method
    4.   Acceleration with an Annual Lump-Sum
    5.   Bi-weekly Payment Plan

1. Flat or Fixed Sum Pre-Payment Plan or Method

In this type of plan, you pay your mortgage lender a fixed, flat amount each month, *in addition* to your required monthly mortgage payment. For example, say you have a 30-year, $100,000 mortgage at 10 percent interest rate, meaning that your normal monthly payment (the principal and interest only, and not including taxes and insurance) is $877.57 (see the Amortization Table on p. 8). You'll simply determine to add in each month an amount you can afford, say $100, to this payment, making the total actual payment $977.57 each month. (Note that, as can be gleaned from Figure 8-1, even this mere payment of this extra $100 per month alone, would save you more than $90,000 in interest costs over the 30-year life of the mortgage, and would let you pay off the loan a little over 10 years sooner.) The sole criterion for picking which amount you may prepay should be what you feel you can afford to pay extra without over-stretching your budget.

Advantages of the Flat-sum Method

The flat-sum prepayment method has several attractive features and advantages. For one thing, this type of plan has the advantage of the element of certainty and predictability; the homeowner involved knows, in advance of each month, exactly how much more money he (or she) will have to be paying, and even more importantly, how much more he can afford to be paying based on his budget. Hence, all you have to do is, first, determine the amount of ADDITIONAL payment you can realistically afford without stretching yourself and your budget unduly – is it $25, $50, $100, or whatever it is – then build that amount into your regular monthly budget.

Let's say, for an example, that all you will be able to save per month, all you'll be able to afford, is $25. You'll add that amount as a pre-payment amount to your regular monthly mortgage payment ($877.57 in the above example) each month, making the total payment you'll send in each month $902.57, and continue paying this amount month after month until the mortgage is paid off.

This additional amount, clearly less than the cost of an evening dinner-out for one person, is a fairly small amount that would hardly pose any hardship on the average homeowner. Yet, by adding just such meager sum to your regular monthly mortgage payment, the effects could still be phenomenal in terms of the interest savings you'll make on your mortgage. Or, maybe all you will be able to afford is an additional $50 per month. If that is the case, then all you do is simply add that $50 to the regular monthly mortgage of $877.57; that'll make it a total of $927.57 ($877.57 + $50) you'll have to be paying per month until the mortgage is paid off. Indeed, you may even ask your mortgage lender to work up for you a mortgage amortization table that is based on the new monthly payment figure you've chosen. Such a table will clearly show you how many months/years shall have been lopped off the original term of your loan based on the prepayment level you choose, and how much sooner your loan will be paid up—5, 8, 10, years or whatever.

Figure 8.1 shows, for each rate of interest listed on a 30-year $100,000 mortgage, the amount of interest payment savings you can make by paying $100 per month <u>extra</u> over and above the regular payments, and the length of time by which your mortgage will be paid off sooner.

Mortgage Rate	Interest Payments Saved	Mortgage Paid Off After
8 percent	$62,465	20.2 years
10 percent	$90,515	19.3 years
12 percent	$123,961	18.3 years
14 percent	$162,270	17.2 years

Figure 8-1. The amount of interest you save at various interest rates, on a 30-year, $100,000 10% interest mortgage, by making regular <u>extra</u> payments of $100 per month.

In every type of investment whatsoever, whether it be putting money in a savings account or in making a mortgage payment, *making sure to systematically put aside a specific, definite amount each month is often critical if one is to achieve one's goals, since by and large people do not readily follow through on the plans they make for reaching a goal.* Hence, as a practical matter, consistently adding a constant, fixed-sum each month is a critical element which makes for the workability and successful implementation of the fixed-sum prepayment method of mortgage acceleration. Once the monthly figure is fixed, there is no further decision to be made. You simply keep to the decision, month after month.

A second advantage of the flat-sum method is somewhat psychological. The mere act of putting aside a fixed-sum each month has the psychological effect – and advantage – of constituting a habit. Since you do not have to make a decision each month regarding making the extra payment (you already know how much you're going to be paying each month), you may not feel the burden of parting with the money each month.

Most people must necessarily adjust their life-style to suit their available income. So, when you are required to pay, say, $500 monthly on your mortgage, but you voluntarily take a decision out of your own personal sense of self-interest to pay $600, you have psychologically created a specific level of monthly expense for yourself. Hence, as your income rises in the future you do not feel or perceive the additional monthly payment necessarily as a burden because it is already built into your budget and because of the sense of mission you feel to attain a self-interested goal of debt-free ownership you've set for yourself. As one analyst put it, the prime advantage of the fixed-sum prepayment system is that it "has the inertial force built into it, it simply propels you toward your goal of debt-free ownership of home … it is as if your mortgage payments were fixed arbitrarily at a slightly higher level, and you were not told about it. It is a pleasant and profitable way of deceiving yourself."[1]

Finally, fixed-sum prepayment method also has the advantage of simplicity. You simply determine how much more you can afford to prepay each month, and add that to your regular payments for each month.

2. Principal-Only (Variable-Sum) Prepayment Method

In a principal-only prepayment plan, you do not pay a set amount extra each month; rather, all you do is pay each month the next month's PRINCIPAL amount due (in addition to your regular monthly payment), and since, *for each month, it will be the PRINCIPAL due on your payment for the next month that you'll have to pay, the amount you prepay each month will VARY*. And because the pre-payment amount you'll pay each month will vary from month to month, this method is also called the "Variable-Sum" Plan. In fact, as we shall see shortly in this Section, this variable amount will gradually but surely increase each month as more and more of your monthly payment becomes applied to the PRINCIPAL.

Essentially, the cornerstone of the principal-only prepayment plan is the prepayment of an amount – comprised of the PRINCIPAL due on the next payment – as determined directly from the monthly Mortgage Amortization Schedule or Table.

To embark on this prepayment plan, first you would need to obtain a "Mortgage Amortization Schedule or Table" that specifically applies to your loan. It's a routine matter, quite easy to secure. In fact, when your mortgage is issued, your lender might usually have given you an amortization schedule, but in the event that he didn't, simply ask for one from any of these sources: your mortgage lender, a bookstore that carries financial paperback books, your loan officer who helped you in your mortgage application and its processing, or even a real estate agent, your bank, or other banks. Also, with an access to a personal computer you can print out an amortization table by punching in the relevant data. Basically, the type of amortization table you need for your loan is a table that shows the monthly payments that'll be necessary to fully amortize (i.e, pay off) your mortgage over the loan term based on the amount of your loan, its interest rate, and the term of the loan, and breaks down your monthly payments into TWO main components, the one going towards the INTEREST, and the one going towards the PRINCIPAL, with the last column showing the unpaid balance still remaining. [See sample Amortization Schedule on p. 8. Others are listed in Appendices B & C.]

What is it that you need an amortization table for? With this table in hand, you will simply be able to determine, each month, the amount you need to pre-pay. Here's how the method works.

---

[1] Vijay Fadia, *How To Cut Your Mortgage in Half: The Homeowner's Guide To Mortgages, Interest & Taxes* (Homestead Publishing Co.) 1990 pp. 47-8

Follow closely the illustration in Figure 8-2 below, and you can see these key relevant information, among others: the amount of the PRINCIPAL you'll be prepaying each month; how much each prepaid principal is SAVING you in interest expense; the BALANCE that's still owed and left to be paid with each month's payment.

ILLUSTRATION: How a Variable Sum (Principal-Only) Prepayment Plan Works

To illustrate how this method works, follow the partial amortization schedule for a sample loan shown in Table 8-2 below.

Loan amount (principal):................................. $100,000
Interest rate:.. 10 percent
Term, number of monthly payments....................30 years, 360 payments
Monthly payment..$877.57
Total interest, if not prepaid............................$215,925
Total cash outlay ($100,000 + $215,925)..............$315,925

		Payment		
Month	Starting Balance	Principal	Interest	Ending Balance
1	$100,000.00	$ 44.24	$833.33	$99,955.76
2	99,955.76	44.61	832.96	99,911.16
3	99,911.16	44.98	832.59	99,866.18
4	99,866.18	45.35	832.22	99,820.84
5	99,820.84	45.73	831.84	99,775.12
6	99,775.12	46.11	831.46	99,729.02
7	99,729.02	46.49	831.08	99,682.52
8	99,682.52	46.88	830.69	99,635.64
9	99,635.64	47.27	830.30	99,588.38
10	99,588.38	47.67	829.90	99,540.72
↓	↓	↓	↓	↓
351	8,394.96	807.61	69.96	7,587.35
352	7,587.35	814.34	63.23	6,773.01
353	6,773.01	821.13	56.44	5,951.88
354	5,951.88	827.94	49.60	5,123.91
355	5,123.91	834.87	42.70	4,289.04
356	4,289.04	841.83	35.74	3,447.21
357	3,447.21	848.84	28.73	2,598.37
358	2,598.37	855.92	21.65	1,742.45
359	1,742.45	863.05	14.52	870.24
360	870.24	870.24	7.33	-0-

Figure 8-2.Amortization schedule showing Principal, Interest, and Ending Balance Break-downs.

Following Table 8-2 closely, you can see that the monthly payment for this $100,000 loan amount for a 30-year term at 10% rate of interest, is $877.57. The schedule shows the first 10 and the last 10 payments, breaking them down between the "principal" and the "interest." If this loan were to be "amortized" (paid off) in the normal way without any prepayment, the total interest cost over the 30-year term, would be $215,925, making the total cash outlay on the home $315,925.

In a variable-sum prepayment plan you can start your prepayment program at any time during the term of the loan, but whenever it is that you choose to start, *what you do is this: simply add the PRINCIPAL payment of the next month to the regular payment of the present month.* Thus, let's say you choose to start from your first payment on the mortgage. From Figure 8-2, we see that the first mortgage payment due is $877.57 ($44.24 + $833.33); so at this time what you do is add the "principal" payment of the second month ($44.61) to the regular payment of $877.57, thereby making it a total of $922.18 you'll need to send in for that month. You may pay it in two separate checks, one for the regular mortgage payment ($877.57, in this case), and the other for the prepayment amount ($44.61 for this month in this case); or, you may pay it in one check. But in either case be sure to include a note with clear instructions as to how you wish your check applied.

Now, continuing with the prepayment plan, next month (Month #2), when you send in your regular monthly payment of $877.57, the extra amount (the prepayment amount) you'll need to add will be the PRINCIPAL for the 3rd month's payment, which is $44.98. Why? Because you have already paid off the principal due for the 2nd month when you made the 1st month's payment. And for month #3, you would add extra payment of $45.35, which is the principal due in Month #4, and so on.

Notice what has happened here with these two sets of payments. By paying as extra in the first month, the principal due for the second month's payment, in the amount of $44.61, you've saved yourself $832.96 in interest cost associated with the second payment; YOU'LL NEVER HAVE TO PAY THAT $832.96 now. And by making the second extra payment of $44.98 (i.e. by pre-paying it) in the second month, you've saved yourself $ 832.59 in interest charges associated with the third month's payment – a combined return of $1,665.58 for the two extra payments of $89.59! But that's not all the savings you've made yourself by this. In addition, by merely making those two extra payments of the principal, alone, you have also chopped two months off the life of the loan – YOU'LL OWN YOUR HOME DEBT-FREE THAT MUCH SOONER. Indeed, if you were to keep it up and dutifully send in one such extra prepayment check each month with each regular monthly payment, you'll cut the life of the mortgage in HALF by that alone, paying off your mortgage in 15 instead of 30 years!

What if there are some months in which you find yourself unable to make the extra payments? Then, you simply don't prepay for those months. You can simply make your regular mortgage payment of $877.57 for that month (or those months); and whenever you happen to come by some extra cash for particular months in the future, you could make a prepayment of your mortgage principal to further save yourself tremendous interest costs.

NOTE: Note that, as a rule, to achieve the maximum savings you would need to do so by starting the prepayment plan as SOON as possible since it is during the EARLIER stages of the loan term that the larger portion of your payments are applied towards the interest charges, rather than to the principal. As can be quickly noticed by looking at Figure 8-2, during the earlier stages of the loan term, a far larger portion of your monthly payment goes to the interest charges, and it is only towards the latter part of the loan term that a large portion of the monthly payment goes towards reducing the principal (the actual loan amount).

Tracking Your Pre-Payments In A Variable Sum Prepayment Method

Since the amount of the principal you prepay each month will vary under this type of prepayment plan, one important question for you may be how do you keep track of the prepayments you make and, more particularly, the savings you make, for each prepayment? And how do you keep track of the progress you are making towards that much-desired goal of paying off your mortgage much sooner?

First, right off the bat one very helpful thing you can do, is don't ever wait until near the end of your mortgage term to make sure you've gotten credit for the extra payments you make. Make it a habit. Once a year, be sure to request a statement from your lender showing how much in principal and interest you paid during the year, and the balance still remaining on the mortgage. Always check the statement carefully to be sure that it accurately reflects the prepayments you did make. [See Chapter 9 for a full discussion of this]

Beside this, here's what you can do on your own. From the same Amortization Table you use to determine the amount you are to prepay for each relevant month (Figure 8-2), you can prepare a special Amortization Table Worksheet which contains columns to enter the "prepayments" and "interest saved", as shown in Figure 8-3 below. On the Worksheet, you enter the following information taken from the amortization schedule: the payment numbers (for a 30-year mortgage, for example, you'll have the number running from 1 to 360), the principal, the interest, and the ending (unpaid) balance amounts. If your prepayment program is started later down the road sometimes after the start of the mortgage payment and you have fewer remaining payments left on your mortgage at that time, then your worksheet should only show the remaining payments, broken down between the principal, interest, and unpaid balance.

EXAMPLE: Let's say your first mortgage payment is June 1st, and that you are in a position to make one prepayment attributed to the month of July. You would enter July 1 in the "Date Paid" column for payments #6 and #7; in the "Amount Paid" column for June, you'll enter $877.57 and for July you'll enter $46.49. You'll also enter $831.08 in the "Interest Saved" column for July. To know how much you shall have saved in interest from the whole prepayment program, simply total up all amounts entered in the column titled "Total Interest Saved."

You would repeat the same process in the month of July. Let's say you make two more prepayments, for the principal amount attributed to August and September—$46.88 and $47.27, respectively. You would make this entry accordingly, as shown in the Worksheet. This is simply the procedure. Each month, when you pay your mortgage, look through your mortgage amortization schedule, determine whether the principal due for the given month is such that you can afford to prepay it, then make the entries in the worksheet accordingly.

Principal-only (Variable Sum) Prepayment Plan
Worksheet

Payment No.	Date Paid	Interest	Interest Saved	Total Interest Saved	Principal	Amount Paid	Unpaid Balance
1							
2							
3							

Figure 8-3. Principal-only Prepayment Plan Worksheet

A Drawback of The Variable Sum Prepayment Plan

Finally, it is worth noting that there is one major drawback associated with the variable sum prepayment method, namely: a special feature of this plan is that as your payments on the mortgage progress, the prepayment amounts (i.e., the principal amounts) you're supposed to be making will no longer remain small, but gradually grow larger and larger with each payment, and will also not be saving you quite as much in interest as the earlier payments did. Indeed, your prepayments will become dramatically larger and larger from just about the time you pass the halfway point of your mortgage term, and at some point further down the way you may find that the prepayments are now so big in size that having to come up with the prepayment amounts on top of the regular monthly payment is now darned well difficult. The reason you have this phenomenon of rapidly increasing size in the prepayment amounts (and the corresponding decrease in the savings you make on each prepayment), is because, given the way the amortization table is structured, it is at that later period in the amortization schedule that a greater portion of our payments goes towards paying off the PRINCIPAL, while a proportionately smaller portion goes towards paying the INTEREST.

Consequently, one realistic drawback of the variable sum prepayment plan you should be prepared to confront is that in the later years further down the amortization road, your prepayments would far outgrow its earlier 'spare change' status and become quite steep; prepayments will, as one analyst sums it up, "no longer be fun; it turns into a daunting task." Indeed, at that point in later years, adhering to such a mortgage plan may mean almost double the original payment! What do you do at such a stage? One option that is certainly open to you, is that you may always cut back on your prepayment then. There is, after all, no obligation under the terms of your mortgage that you must make any extra payments other than your regular payments. Hence, if at some point during your prepayment program under this plan you find yourself no longer in a position to prepay, that's just fine. You can stop for a certain period of time, or for any month, and prepay in any month you find yourself with some extra cash to spare. The choice is entirely yours.

3.   Fixed-Term Prepayment Plan Or Method

A third kind of prepayment method we shall address here by which one may undertake his mortgage acceleration goal, is a fixed term prepayment plan. Basically, what you do under this method is to determine the mortgage pay-off date you desire – the length of time you'd want by which to repay or pay off your mortgage – and then calculate the amount you'd need to be paying each month in order to reach that goal.

Ideally, the prepayment amount you go with should be something you can reasonably afford over the duration of the pay-off period chosen. However, under this prepayment plan even if right now you cannot readily afford the payment that's required to meet that goal, you may simply pay what you can at the moment. Factored into this, is a fairly reasonable assumption that financial conditions will change favorably (or at least not get worse) for you in the future, and that you might well reach your goal by adjusting your payment (upwards) again and again in the future, as warranted, to make the goal.

ILLUSTRATION: Assume, for an example, that you have a $100,000, 30-year, fixed-rate mortgage at 10 percent interest (it must be a conventional, fixed-rate mortgage for a fixed term prepayment method to be feasible). That will mean that your monthly payments (see the Amortization Table on p. 8) are $877.58, and you'll be paying approx. $215,928 in total interest over the 360-month life of the mortgage. Now, let's say that what you rather do is cut down the life of the mortgage and pay it all off in, say, 25 years, or 20 years or 15 years, rather than 30 years. How do you determine the prepayment amount you will require (or the savings you stand to make) for the goal you choose? It's simple. Look up the figures from any one of the many mortgage amortization tables that are generally available from public libraries and the average stationery store. Look for the "Monthly Payment Necessary To Amortize A Loan" type of table, such as the tables reproduced in Appendix B. Frequently, you may also be able to obtain such a table that'll fit your particular purposes from your mortgage bank or lending institution (simply request one from your loan officer who helped you with your loan application and processing). [Refer, also, to Chapter 9 for the general details about figuring out and calculating your payments]

Here are some sample calculations:

Figure 8-4. Fixed Term Prepayment Schedule: Monthly Payments Necessary To Amortize Loan

Amount of Loan: $100,000
Interest rate: 10 percent

Term of Loan	Monthly Payment	Total Payment	Total Interest	You save This in Interest
30 years	$877.58 (360 months)	$315,928	$215,928	----
25 "	$908.71 (300 months)	$272,613	$172,613	$43,315
20 "	$965.03 (240 months)	$231,607	$131,607	$84,321
15 "	$1,074.61 (180 months)	$193,430	$ 93,430	$122,498
10 "	$1,321.51 (120 months)	$158,581	$ 58,581	$157,347

An important advantage of the fixed term prepayment system, is its cheer simplicity. You simply determine the length of time by which you want to pay off your mortgage and own your home free and clear, and your monthly payments are fixed based on that term. And, providing the monthly pre-payment amount you choose is one you feel comfortable with and can afford, you would be able to speed up your mortgage repayment and own your home debt-free some five, ten, fifteen, or so years sooner, as calculated. For example, let's say your choice is to pay off your mortgage in 20 years. Then, from Table 8-4 above (or from a table like Appendix B), you can determine what it will take in terms of monthly payments to accomplish that ($965.03); and, assuming you can afford that amount (an extra $87.45 per month over the monthly regular of $877.58 for the 30-year term), that's the payment schedule you'd stick to.

> *Note*: Note that fixed term prepayment plans are applicable only with conventional, FIXED-TERM mortgages. With adjustable rate mortgages, fixed term prepayments are simply not practicable as you'll have to change your payments every time there is an adjustment in the interest rate.

4. Acceleration With an Annual Lump-Sum Payment

Another type of prepayment method a homeowner can employ, is to make a regular prepayment of lump-sum amounts. Many homeowners, already strained from month to month on other family expenses, lack the resources to allow for any flexibility, and some may find, even after a lot of disciplined budgeting and careful planning, that adding an extra payment on top of the existing family budget, is just too much of a burden to bear, at least immediately.

Given that situation, one viable alternative might be to use your annual income tax refund to accelerate the mortgage. Merely adding a $1,000 refund amount annually to your mortgage, for example, (based on a 30-year $80,000 loan at 10% interest), will reduce your repayment term by 224 months or 18 years and 8 months; and adding just a $300 refund annually to your mortgage is equivalent to making extra $25 payment per month towards your mortgage, and will take as much as 5 years off your repayment term. And so on and so forth, with different amounts.

Note: For this plan to really work and yield you the usual substantial benefits of serious mortgage prepayment, such lump-sum payments must be *constant* and regularly made, attended with dedication and a sense of purpose till the mortgage is finally paid off.

5. The Bi-Weekly Payment Method

The final type of pre-payment method we shall consider, is the bi-weekly payment plan. Simply put, the term "bi-weekly" means EVERY TWO WEEKS. There are 52 weeks in every year, hence a bi-weekly payment plan implies a plan whereby you make your payments bi-weekly (every two weeks), rather than every month, or twice a month, and the like. In a bi-weekly mortgage payment method, a borrower typically makes 26 payments in each year, as opposed to the merely the usual 12 monthly payments. *This basically means that you take the annual mortgage amount you pay and simply divide it up in such a way that it comes out to your writing a check EVERY TWO WEEKS, rather than once per month, or even twice per month.*

There are a few ways you can accomplish this. You can, for example, do this: take your usual monthly mortgage payment amount and split it into half, then take that half-month rate and pay that every two weeks. To put it another way, you take what you have to pay monthly (your regular monthly mortgage payment) and simply split it in half; and then start paying that half month's amount every two weeks – rather than making one full month's payment every month. Or, another way of mechanically doing the same thing is this: since there are 26 two-week periods in a year, you simply divide your regular annual mortgage amount by 26 and that's what you pay each and every two weeks until your mortgage is fully liquidated.*

BUT HERE'S REALLY THE SIGNIFICANT POINT ABOUT THIS METHOD. When you pay once *every two weeks*, that amounts to making 26 half payments per year, and when you make 26 half payments for the year, that's 13 full payments (13 full month's worth) for the year. To put it another way, what this basically means, is that because there are 52 weeks in the year, the mere fact that you pay bi-weekly (every two weeks), instead of merely every month, directly translates into your making 26 half payments per year, which means 13 FULL MONTHS payments for the year. That is, instead of payments amounting to just 12 full months of mortgage payments for the year, you would have made payments which amount to 13 FULL MONTHS worth! That's equal to one ADDITIONAL month's payment per year. That one extra month's payment you make each year is applied toward your loan's principal, thereby reducing the repayment term and saving you tremendous interest charges over the term of the loan.

Perhaps you are paid once every two weeks, any way (instead of either twice per month or monthly.) In that case, each of your 26 bi-weekly mortgage payments for the year will automatically fall into your bi-weekly pay periods. Or, you may be paid either monthly or semi-monthly (twice per month). In either situation, you can try to budget your paycheck and schedule it so that you pay one-half of the regular monthly mortgage every other week (every

---

* There's yet another way one can do this: divide your regular monthly payment by 12 and send in that extra amount each month along with your regular payment. At the end of a year, the 12 payments will equal one extra month's payment, all of which goes towards reducing the principal. For example, assume your mortgage is $125,000 at 7.75 percent for a 30-year term, and your required monthly payment is $896. Divide the $896 by 12, and you get $75. Add that $75 to your regular monthly payment, and that's how much ($971) you'll need to be sending in each and every month – and you'll save yourself over $40,000 in interest and slice 8 years off your mortgage just by doing that.

two weeks). And if you do this, you will wind up making 26 half payments in a year (that's how many two-week periods there are in a year since there are 52 weeks in a year), which means 13 full payments per year. This means that, for each year, you would wind up PRE-PAYING one extra month's regular mortgage payment (13 full month's payments, as opposed to 12), and that extra payment each year gets applied, of course, toward the mortgage principal.

This one extra payment per year alone would result in a tremendous reduced interest costs to you as a borrower, and speedier pay-off of the mortgage. How tremendous and how much speedier? That one extra payment per year alone, will reduce a 30-year loan, for example, to between 18 and 20 years for repayment – just that alone is sufficient, in other words, to cut the time of your repayment by 10 to 12 years, or more than one-third of the whole term.

ILLUSTRATION: Assume you have a 30-year, $115,000 mortgage borrowed at 10% interest rate. Your monthly loan payment under such terms (see Appendix B) would be $1,009.21, and you would have had to pay $248,316 in total interest cost over the 30-year life of the mortgage.

But now, let's say you change the payment schedule and make it into BI-WEEKLY payments, instead of MONTHLY. This would mean that you'll need to be paying $504.61 (one-half of the monthly $1,009.21) and be doing so every 2 weeks, meaning that at the end of every one year period you would be making an equivalent of one more extra month's regular payment. The result of this one extra month's payment each year would be the following: your total interest payable is reduced from $248,316 to $158,193, which is a savings of $90,123; the loan will be paid off in 18 years, compared to 30 years, meaning you'll own your home 12 years sooner.

Figure 8-5. Interest and time savings made through bi-weekly payments on a $150,000 mortgage at 8.5%, 30-year fixed term.

	Regular mortgage	Bi-weekly mode
Paid off in:	30 years	22.5 years
Total interest:	$265,217.00	$187,607.00
Interest savings:	None	$77,610.00
No. of payments saved:	None	89 months
Gross payment savings:	None	$102,651.00
Average yearly interest savings:	None	$3,437.00

C. The Popular Appeal Of The Bi-Weekly Payment Method Today

In recent times, many private companies and business organizations, big and small, some of whom have made huge financial fortunes marketing the concept, have sprung up all across the nation to offer varying mortgage acceleration services to homeowners – for a fee, of course. Promoted by different organizations under various names – such as "Bi-weekly Mortgage Program," "Mortgage Reduction Program," or "Mortgage Acceleration Program" – the programs offered by such commercial enterprises purport to arrange, on behalf of the homeowner for a set fee, a bi-weekly payment plan directly with the mortgage bank or lender. Basically, you (the homeowner) will sign up with the company, which then acts as a go-between for you and your mortgage lender. Usually, for a one-time fee paid by the homeowner (the typical amount as of

1998 is $395), the company offers electronic fund transfers by which to make your mortgage payments for you with your lender. Rather than you having to send a check to your bank each month to make your mortgage payment, you send the company the monthly amount and the company, in turn, then sends your bank, every two weeks, the appropriate amount equivalent to one-half of your monthly payment. Or, in the alternative, the company could simply debit your checking account (or savings account) every two weeks for an amount equal to one-half of your regular monthly payment, and then remit the equivalents to your mortgage lender every two weeks.

And what does the acceleration service company get from you for this rather simple service? It gets paid rather handsomely for it. In three ways. First, you pay him the initial "set up" fee of some $400 to $500 up front, then an on-going service fee of about $2 or $3 per payment each month. And finally, depending on the service company you deal with, the company would often earn interest (some do, but others would credit you with the interest) on your money for two weeks of every month.

Are The Services Offered By The Mortgage Acceleration Service Companies Worth It?
Critics have emerged and now abound, however, who cast serious doubt on everything from the intrinsic value of the service performed by the mortgage acceleration service companies, to its legitimacy and the economic wisdom of paying them for it. Principally, the basic question by most of the critics boils down to this: why pay a company for such a service when you can accomplish the same thing just as well on your own? Critics of the need for the private mortgage acceleration companies, or the usefulness of the service they provide, contend basically that the homeowner need no go-between with their lenders, that they can just as well, for example, simply mail the lender one extra half payment of their monthly mortgage twice a year, the same as the mortgage acceleration service companies do, anyway, but without having to incur their fees and charges.

Indeed, the mortgage acceleration service companies themselves, generally acknowledge that homeowners could just as easily make the bi-weekly mortgage payments on their own, dealing directly with their banks and lenders. HOMEOWNERS CAN DO SO QUITE ALRIGHT, THE SERVICE COMPANIES ASSERT. BUT THEY JUST WOULDN'T. Rather, if left entirely to the homeowner's initiative to do it, the service providers say, what the homeowner is all too likely to do, is to use that extra money for other expenses, instead. The value and purpose the company brings to the table, they contend, is that they provide self-discipline, consistency and structure to the process. The mortgage acceleration service companies argue that it is the fact that they provide the homeowner with regularly scheduled payment plan that more or less makes possible the realization of great interest savings for the homeowner over time on the homeowner's mortgage.

For our purposes here, suffice it to say that the underlying posture taken by the acceleration service companies is not without some strong element of validity and reality in it. IN TRUTH, IN THE FINAL ANALYSIS, THE SUCCESS OF ANY HOMEOWNER WITH ANY KIND OF MORTGAGE ACCELERATION PROGRAM WILL DEPEND ON SELF-DISCIPLINE. *To succeed, you must have— the basic, indispensable presumption is that you'll have— enough self-discipline to stay persevering and focused, and to stick to the chosen financial goal and pre-*

payment plan. Self-discipline is, in a word, the critical intangible, the necessary and indispensable condition that is presumed present in any payment acceleration plan, without which acceleration plan can not succeed.

It is fair to presume, however, that homeowners, especially when they've become fully acquainted with the basic information about the workings of mortgage acceleration and the awesome financial rewards that can accrue to them through mortgage acceleration, are equally capable of the essential self-discipline necessary for a successful acceleration program. Consequently, this response by one analyst to the issue of whether or not the services of the mortgage acceleration companies are, indeed, essential, seems perhaps most apt: "It's open to question, however, how valuable this service really is. If you have enough money to pay ahead on your mortgage, you'd do best to make your own arrangements with your lender, and not waste money on a middleman."[*]

Additionally, perhaps the bi-weekly payment method is already convenient and better suited for you, any way, if you happen to be among the large number of employed persons who are paid bi-weekly, rather than semi-monthly or monthly. According to one study, about one-half of all the employees in the United States are paid bi-weekly. For homeowners falling under such category, all they'll need to do then would be simply to budget their mortgage payment out of each paycheck (preferably the same amount each time) and send it in to their lender.

In fact, just for a general sense of how readily easy it could be for the average homeowner to use the bi-weekly payment plan in paying off his mortgage loan, you can throw away all the elaborate thoughts and ideas you've ever heard about the formal mechanics of "bi-weekly" payment, and simply do this: JUST MAKE ONE EXTRA FULL MONTH'S MORTGAGE PAYMENT AT THE BEGINNING OF EACH YEAR. And just by doing this alone, you would have accelerated even at a better rate than you'll achieve with any formal bi-weekly program – but without the regimentation, or the possible expense, of a bi-weekly mortgage payment process! With that one extra month's payment alone each year, you'll achieve a cut of 10 to 12 years in the length of time it'll take you to repay a 30-year loan, dramatically bringing the repayment time down from 30 years to between 18 and 20 years!

---

[*] John R, Dorfman, *The Mortgage Book* (Consumer Reports Books) p. 188

CHAPTER 9
TO DERIVE THE MAXIMUM BENEFITS FROM YOUR PREPAYMENT PROGRAM, YOU MUST PERSONALLY KEEP A CLOSE TRACK OF YOUR PAYMENTS

A. Why Keeping Track, Personally, Is Of Such Critical Importance For You

In the preceding Chapter 8, the many different ways and methods by which prepayments can be made are outlined. As fully explained, you may choose to do it on a regular, planned basis; or, you can make only occasional extra payments. *Whichever type of plan you prefer or employ, however, and whatever the mechanics involved in the plan used, if you are to get the maximum benefit out of your prepayment effort, there is one fundamental imperative you must comply with, namely: you must maintain, by and for yourself, a reliable and systematic way by which to police and keep a close track of all your payments. You must act as a watchdog to track your payments on your own behalf.*

Why is this so necessary? Only by keeping a close track, yourself, of the payments you make, can you be certain—can you guarantee—that you get full credit for the totality of the payments you make, for, believe it or not, the credible evidence available is that banks and lenders can, and do, make mistakes in their calculations, even when they are done by computers!

To be sure, the bookkeeping required to keep track of your prepayments, while generally not complex, could often be confusing. As a practical matter, probably because of this, most homeowners entrust the task of handling the mortgage payment math and bookkeeping to their lenders, trusting them to keep track of the ever-shifting amortized balances that remain outstanding with each payment or prepayment. But this attitude, while understandable, is not quite wise or advisable. The problem, simply, is that lenders can, and do, make mistakes in their calculations. Several reports by investigators and various government agencies abound, for example, which have shown lenders making numerous serious errors in their calculations of borrowers' payments, particularly under adjustable mortgages. True, lender errors are rare and not a common, every-day occurrence. But they do, in the real world, happen from time to time. And, when they do happen, they are often very expensive errors for the borrower! Sure, banks and mortgage lenders have a reputation for having the most sophisticated internal accounting and control systems and automated computer processes. Still, they are prone to human errors— computers are programmed by human beings, they are run and are fed information by flawed humans, like you and I!

THUS, A FAR BETTER BUT ADVISABLE STRATEGY FOR YOU, IS: you let your mortgage lender carry on with the routine bookkeeping for your payments, but be sure to police and verify their work for accuracy to be certain that the proper credits and adjustments were made by the lender. You're more in control when you track the lender's calculations and compare them to your own.

Here are the few simple procedures. In the first place, be sure not to wait until the end of your mortgage term to verify that you've been given full credit for your extra payments. Quite to the contrary, start making your verification of the lender's calculations from the very first year of your prepayment program. At the end of the first year of making prepayments, and then once every year thereafter, have your lender send you (specifically ask them to send you) a statement of account tabulating all the payments you've made for the preceding year and showing how much PRINCPAL and how much INTEREST you paid for that year, and the remaining BALANCE. Upon your receiving that statement, promptly check the figures; verify that they reflect all the payments you have made. [A simple formula to use: the Principal, plus the Interest payments reported in the lender's statement, should add up to 12 times your regular monthly payments, plus the extra payments. And your outstanding balance reported each year in the lender's statement shall have declined by all the regular principal payments made for the year, plus the extra payments.]

The process of practically calculating the mortgage payments in terms of the principal, the interest, and the outstanding balances, is not at all complex or sophisticated. Indeed, figuring out loan amortization process requires only a few, simply steps. *There are, of course, computers, even hand-held calculators, that you could have do all the work for you. However, to understand how the amortization process actually works, it is strongly advisable that you go through the steps for yourself. Doing so will eliminate any sense of mystery about the process for you, putting you in control not only over your mortgage, but over your other finances.*

B. Here's How To Calculate The Principal, The Interest Payments, & The Balance

Concerning calculating the interest payment, the basic interest formula involves the principal, an interest rate, a compounding method, and time. The "principal" is the outstanding debt; the "interest" rate is expressed on an ANNUAL basis. Hence, to get the MONTHLY interest, you have to divide the annual rate by 12 (months).

Let's take an example of 11 percent per year, compounded monthly. To calculate the <u>monthly</u> interest (as opposed to the yearly interest), you'll divide the annual rate (11%) by 12, as follows:

$$\frac{11.00\%}{12} = .917\%$$

We'll convert this monthly interest percentage to its decimal form (we need to do this in order to be able to figure this using a calculator), you simply move the decimal point two places to the left. The .917% percent then becomes .00917 in decimal form.

Next, let's assume your mortgage is $100,000. You refer to the Amortization Table in Appendix B. You find that a $100,000, 11% mortgage amortized over 30 years will require a monthly payment of $952.33.

This ($952.33) is the monthly payment. Now, how does this monthly payment of $952.33 break down in interest, and in principal, for a given month. First, to figure the INTEREST portion, the monthly interest rate is applied against the outstanding loan balance, so you need only to multiply that loan balance by the monthly rate, as follows:

$100,000 X .00917 = $917 (the 1st month's interest portion of the payment)

Next, to figure the PRINCIPAL portion, you simply subtract the interest part from the total monthly payment, as follows:

Total monthly payment	$953.33
Less: interest portion	-917.00
Principal payment portion	$ 36.33

Thus, the principal payment for the first month of this loan is just $36.33. To get the loan's NEW BALANCE, you reduce the existing balance by this principal payment, as follows:

$100,000.00
-          36.33
New balance $ 99,963.67

The second month's payment will be only slightly more to principal and slightly less to interest, as follows: (The 2nd month's INTEREST part of the monthly payment is $99,963.67 X .00917, which is equal to $916.67)

Hence the calculation for this (the 2nd) month is,

Total monthly payment	$953.33
Less: Interest portion	-916.67
Principal payment	$ 36.66

Loan's new balance, is $99,963.67 - $36.66, which is $99,927.01

Using the Worksheet To Make Your Calculations

The worksheet below, Figure 9-1, shows in a worksheet format, essentially the same steps by which you may break down your monthly payments into its principal, interest, and the ending balance. The same set of facts apply: the mortgage loan is for $100,000, at 11 percent interest rate to be amortized over a 30 year term. The calculation starts with the very first month of the loan payment.

C. Tracking Your Debt Repayments, Step-By-Step

As previously emphasized, you should keep a close, running tab on your mortgage payments. Most preferably, you should track them MONTHLY. Depending on the particular reporting policy followed by your lender, your lender may give you its report of your outstanding balance, and a breakdown of your payments, each month or each quarter. Some may do so only at the end of each year. In any case, if your lender does not make its report frequently, say monthly or quarterly, then write your lender a special letter demanding a report of your payments and your debt status at least every quarter. Do a calculation of your own on a monthly basis. Keep a running record of it with a workbook, such as the one shown in Figure 9-2. Each month, you enter the date and amount of your payment, including any prepayment made for that month, under the appropriate columns as in Figure 9-2, and enter the mortgage balance from one month to another.

Worksheet: Loan Payments

1. Enter the balance of the loan $100,000

2. Multiply by the interest rate
   (in decimal form)   x   .11

3. Result: annual interest $ 11,000

4. Divide by 12   ÷ 12

5. Result: this month's interest $ 916.67

6. Subtract the monthly payment   − 952.33

7. Result: this month's principal   − $ 35.66

8. Add the loan balance forward   + 100,000

9. Result: new loan balance $ 99,964.34

Figure 9-1. Worksheet: Breakdown of Payment Into Interest, Principal & Balance.

Mortgage Record

Lender _____

Address _____

City_____

Telephone _____

Contact Person _____

Loan Number _____ Interest Rate _____

DATE	PAYMENT	INTEREST	PRINCIPAL	BALANCE

Figure 9-2. Record of Mortgage Payments

Then, simply compare your own figures to those of your lender. This way, you'll be sure that your lender applied your regular payments, as well as your extra payments, correctly. Physically doing the calculations yourself and comparing them to the lender's figures to make sure that all your payments are correctly and timely applied, puts you in control of your own finances. Otherwise, you'll always be having yourself at the mercy of the lender's computers, and always dependent on whatever the lender reports to you. A simple lender's error that you may catch, for example, could potentially mean saving yourself thousands of dollars that can mean a big difference in determining how long your loan is amortized, especially when you've taken all the trouble and made all the self sacrifice to undertake an acceleration payment program.

D. Using The Amortization Tables To Track Your Debt

A general way of calculating the amount of interest and principal that should be applied to your loan each month, is by using the interest Amortization Table. Different types of interest tables, about six in number, exist. Each of the different tables serves a particular purpose. However, for purposes of mortgage management, you need only know just one table.

Each type of table would identify the distinct compounding method used (e.g., the tables in Appendix B, indicate that the compounding is done "monthly", not quarterly or otherwise.) Each table will clearly identify an interest rate; the various amounts of required payment, based on the loan amount; and the repayment term in years.

a) The Amount-Listed Types of Table

Now, refer to the tables set forth in Appendix B. It lists a series of interest amortization tables. Each table is compounded monthly at stated rates of interest, and includes a number of different loan amounts up to $100,000. Amount listed tables, such as the type of tables listed in Appendix B, deal purely with the actual amount of monthly payments required to amortize a loan. These kinds of tables are often called "payment necessary to amortize a loan" tables.

The major advantage of this type of table is that, at a glance, you can easily see how payments change over time. However, a major inconvenience of the amount-listed tables, is that, because not every amount can be listed, when the amount of a loan is not specifically listed you'll have to add two or more different payments together to arrive at the amount required.

EXAMPLE: Let's say you're looking for a mortgage loan for $53,550, at 10% for a 30-year term. How do you figure what should be the monthly payment using the appropriate amount-listed table? Now, refer to Appendix B, and you'll need to add together from the proper table therein several amounts as follows:

Monthly payment necessary to amortize a loan ($53,550, 30-year, 10%)

Amount	Monthly Payment
$50,000	$438.79
20,000	17.56
1,000	8.78
500	4.39
50	.44
$53,550	$469.96

b) Factor-Listed Types Of Table

A factor-listed table is the type that offers factors rather than amounts. The basic advantage of these types of tables is that it solves the above state problem of not being able to get the required amount of monthly payment when the loan involved is not specifically listed in the table. To get the monthly payment, a factor is simply multiplied by the loan amount, and the result is the monthly payment required.

The major advantage of the factor-listed type of tables, is that it is easy to use for calculations in a situation involving odd amounts. But factor tables are less easy to use for scanning and comparing rates and payment levels from one interest rate to another, or from one loan amount or repayment term to another. Hence, for the purposes of studying the difference in rates, repayment terms, and amounts borrowed, the amount-listed tables have the advantage, but for fast calculations of odd amounts, the factor-listed tables have the advantage.

The factors in factor-listed tables look like this, assuming a 10 percent interest rate, compounded monthly:

Years	Factors	Years	Factors
21	0.0095078	22	0.0093825
23	0.0092718	24	0.0091739
25	0.0090870	26	0.0090098
27	0.0089410	28	0.0088796
29	0.0088248	30	0.0087757

ILLUSTRATION: Let's assume exactly the same figures as in the previous example: the mortgage loan is for $53,550 at 10 percent interest for a 30-year term. How do you figure what should be the monthly payment using the factor-listed table? You simply multiply the amount involved by the factor in the row for 30 years, as follows:

$$\$53,550 \times 0.0087757 = \$469.94$$

c) How You May Have To Estimate The Right Amount When The Exact Interest Rate Is Not Listed In The Table

There's one more potential problem you may come across in your using an amortization table to work out the monthly payment: the exact interest rate for your loan may not be listed on the book of amortization table you are using. Generally, the books of amortization table available will contain interest rates at ¼ percent intervals—that is, they will have rates of, say, 10 percent, 10.25, 10.5, 10.75 and 11.0 percent, but will not have any percentage in between. They will not, for example, have any rates at 1/8 percent intervals—such as 10.125 percent, 10.375, 10.625, or 10.875 percent.

How do you work out from the table what the monthly payment should be in such a situation when the loan rate quoted you by your lender is at 1/8 percent intervals, but the table you have only has rates at ¼ intervals? Simply, the way you work this out, is by what is called "interpolation"—approximating of the proper payment. This can be done using either a payment-listed type of table (Appendix B), or a factor-listed one. But here, we'll use a payment-listed table for our example.

      EXAMPLE: Let's say your lender has quoted you a mortgage loan at an interest rate of 10.125 (10 1/8) percent, and that the amortization book of monthly payments you have shows only 10.0 and 10.25 (10 ¼) percent interest rates. The loan amount is for $100,000 for 30-year term.

To work out the required monthly payments at 10.125 percent interest rate, here are the few simple steps:
1. Find out from the amortization table (Appendix B) the monthly payment at the interest rates above and below the target rate (10.125%). For the rate above, the 10.25 percent payment would be $896.11; and for the rate below, the 10.0 percent payment would be $877.58
2. Get an average of the two payments set forth in step 1 above, as follows:

$$\frac{\$896.11 + \$877.58}{2} = \$886.84$$

Thus, the approximate monthly payment required for a $100,000 loan, to be repaid over 30 years at interest rate of 10.125 percent, is $886.84.

d) The Remaining Balance Type Of Tables, And How To Use Them For Managing Your Mortgage Payment Plan

Finally, there is one other type of table you should know about, which is useful in the management of your mortgage. It's called the REMAINING BALANCE table. Basically, this type of table shows the percentage of a loan that still remains unpaid and outstanding at the end of each year of the loan term. Remaining balance types of table are the types set forth in Appendix C.

Studying the Tables in Appendix C, you'll find that, for purposes of managing your mortgage, the remaining balance table is a useful tool to you in a variety of ways:

- It shows, with graphic clarity, how your mortgage is gradually being paid off over the term of the loan, and what it'll take you to pay off the mortgage. For example, for the 9 percent remaining balance table (Appendix C), you can immediately see, in a graphic way, that for a 30-year loan at the end of the 22nd year, you still have remaining nearly 53 percent of the loan (or, to put it another way, you have only paid off 47% of the loan), and that it is only towards the very tail end of the loan term, in the last 8 years, that the bulk of the loan finally begins to be seriously paid off.

- A remaining balance table could be a great financial planning tool for you: with it, you can determine how and when you'd want to repay your mortgage, or how and when to accelerate payments, and even how and when you may want to refinance your existing mortgage.

- A remaining balance table gives you a fair idea of how much equity you are likely to have available in your home, which is a vital information to have for a refinancing plan in the future. Let's assume, for example, that you plan to refinance your home in 4 years. You'll assume there'll be a given rate of market growth of say, some 4 percent per year for your home, based on the past. So, if you have a fair idea of the current market, the remaining balance tables give you an idea of how much equity you are likely to have on your home in about the next 4 years.

CHAPTER 10
PAYING OFF YOUR MORTGAGE FAST & STEADY: HERE ARE THE COMPLETE STEP-BY-STEP PROCEDURES TO DO IT, FROM START TO FINISH

To keep the proper and organized perspective on whether or not to undertake a program of mortgage acceleration for your home, and the proper times and circumstances when to do so, and to make proper formulation of how such a program may fit into your overall personal plan, follow the following steps and guidelines step-by-step, systematically, and in the same order as listed below.

A. First Double-Check The Provisions Of Your Mortgage Contract On Prepayments

You should be aware that there are some banks and lenders, though increasingly fewer and rarer in number nowadays, who do not quite take kindly to a borrower prepaying his/her mortgage. The probable basis of their objection about it? Well, for one thing, there are lenders who fear that a large number of their customers may prepay when interest rates are down, and thus deprive them of what would have been an attractive stream of incomes as they'll be compelled to lend out funds at lower interest rates, spelling depressed profits to the lenders.

Hence, a good place to begin for a homeowner contemplating engaging in a program of mortgage acceleration, is to double-check the provisions of his mortgage agreement (the promissory note) relating to prepayment. Does the mortgage note contain any penalties for prepaying the loan, and if so how severe a penalty? Obviously, undertaking a prepayment program for your mortgage can only become more likely for you when there is no serious or costly penalty attached for prepaying.

Fortunately for most homeowners, many states now have laws on the books which prohibit outright any prepayment penalties whatsoever for mortgage payments, while others strictly limit the size or circumstances of the penalties that lenders may impose. Such states include the following: Alabama, Alaska, Illinois, Iowa, Maryland, Minnesota, New Jersey, New Mexico, North Carolina, Pennsylvania, South Carolina, Texas, Vermont, and West Virginia, among others. Indeed, even in many of such instances where penalty is attached to prepaying, frequently such penalty provisions only apply for prepayments made during the first few years (some 2, 3, or 5 years or so) of the loan term.

In any event, the important point to note here is that , one of the very first moves you should make BEFORE you ever start out on a prepayment plan, is to double-check the terms of your mortgage agreement on what it says (or does not say) about prepaying your mortgage.

Furthermore, take a closer look also at the important document know as the "'Truth-in-Lending Statement." By law you shall have received this document from your mortgage lender when you were first granted the loan. This document will fully describe for you any prepayment penalty there may be for your loan, if any.

Finally, if you plan to prepay your mortgage, you should make it your duty to contact your lender (by phone, letter or in person), in any case, to officially inform them of your plans. This way, aside from your being able to confirm from the lender that they will accept your extra payments, you'll also be in a position to discuss with them the mutually acceptable procedures for making the payments, and for their keeping record of your payments—matters such as whether you'd have to make the extra payments in a separate check or to add it in the regular monthly payment; or whether your lender credits your extra payments immediately upon receipt of the check, or at a later time, will be relevant issues that could be discussed, among others. Also, whenever you send in a prepayment check to your lender, its always a good practice to attach a note or letter with specific instructions to the lender to apply the amount towards the PRINCIPAL.

B. Never Accelerate When, Or If, You Can't Afford It

First of all, you should never accelerate your mortgage when you can't afford to do so, in the first place. This will be just one of the very few circumstances when embarking on payment acceleration will be a poor idea on your part. If you are on a tight budget already, and can hardly afford your regular mortgage payments, you should forget acceleration in the meantime. If and when, in the future, your financial situation should improve to a point where you can, with a little convenience, AFFORD paying something additional, you may then consider starting an acceleration plan at that point accordingly—after you shall have FIRST set up a reasonable emergency reserve fund. (See Chapter 2, and Item D below).

C. Design A Payment Plan To Suit Your Particular Budget

A basic rule of any financial plan, is that, for it ever to be practicable and effectual, it must, first and foremost, be workable within the context of what your budget can bear. Hence, an important rule in devising a mortgage acceleration plan is this: *design your plan to be flexible.* If, for example, all you can afford TODAY in extra payment is a modest amount, then structure your payments that way, but provide for revisions in the plan to increase or decrease payments at differing times according to changes in your income and financial circumstances. Acceleration of one's mortgage is deemed one of the most flexible ways by which one can invest: you can design your additional payments to suit you according to your desire, goal, and financial ability, and you can modify your payments as often as you wish or find it necessary. [See pp. 34 & 46]

D. First Set Up An Emergency Reserve Fund BEFORE
Ever Starting An Acceleration Plan

Mortgage payment (and/or its acceleration) is often said to be a very "illiquid" investment – that is, once you invest in your home equity, you cannot readily withdraw or get the money back if you were immediately to need it. Once invested in an equity, the only way you can recover the invested money is practically by borrowing against it (say by refinancing or getting an equity loan), or by selling the house. In effect, it is ill-advised to begin an acceleration program with funds you would need almost soon thereafter. Hence, before you ever undertake an acceleration plan for your mortgage, you had better put aside, FIRST, enough money to take care of potential emergencies that could arise, such as illness, loss of or decrease in family income, and sudden loss of a job, and for allowances for regular payment of property taxes or insurance, etc. You must, in other words, FIRST set up an adequate EMERGENCY RESERVE FUND. Only when – and after – you shall have set up such an emergency reserve fund, would an acceleration of your mortgage make sense, and then become advisable. [See Chapter 2 for details on the setting up of an emergency reserve fund].

E. If You Have To Refinance Your Mortgage, Do So Only On Good, Sensible, Financial Grounds

Refinancing of your mortgage is a form of mortgage acceleration that could be very worthwhile, financially, under the right circumstances. If you undertake this form of acceleration, you must first be absolutely sure you do so under the few limited circumstances when refinancing will make financial sense for you; first, be certain that you've carefully made the calculation and that it makes financial sense in that it actually reduces your interest cost over time; and, second, be certain that the proceeds you'll get upon refinancing is meant for, and will actually be used to improve, enhance, and add to the structure and value of the property [See Chapter 9 for more on this].

F. Choose An Appropriate Type of Pre-Payment Plan For You

There are a few different kinds of pre-payment plans available to the homeowner. Familiarize yourself with the various plans. Then pick one plan (or even a combination of the plans) within the context of what is practicable for you – what best suits your budget and financial goal, your priorities and current financial status. [See Chapter 8, at pp. 49-62, for details about the different types of prepayment plans available and their varying strengths and drawbacks.]

G. As A Prime Element Of Your Plan, Definitely Pick A Specific Pay-Off Date For Your Mortgage

Sure, the mere setting of a goal on any given task or project may be easy – the "easy part." And the actual attainment of that goal may not be as easy. Nevertheless, it's always very helpful to set a goal. Setting a goal is only the very first step. You don't necessarily have to take immediate action if you can't afford to at the moment. It will often help to have a goal, still. Why? Simply because it is only by having a goal that you can begin to find out and map out what you need to do to reach it, and knowing what you need to do to reach a goal would often lead to solutions.

So, set your acceleration goal, anyway, by picking a specific repayment date you'd prefer by which to pay off your mortgage. Let's say you have a 30-year mortgage on a given loan amount (say it's for $100,000), but that you would like to be able to pay off that mortgage in roughly 20 years. Then, first of all, you should find the answer to this vital information: 'how much money in total dollars, would I have to pay in specific terms each month to reach this goal, and how much more in EXTRA dollars per month would that mean I'll have to find over and above my regular monthly mortgage payment?'

Using the appropriate amortization table, you can readily compare various payoff dates for different years; [*] thus, assuming the mortgage is at 9 ¼ percent rate of interest, your normal monthly payment on the 30-year, $100,000 mortgage is $822.68. To attain your goal of paying it off in about 20 years rather than 30 years, you would have to accelerate your required payment from $822.68 to $915.87 per month – some $93.19 in extra money that you'll need to find and afford each month.

Then, the next important question for you will be: 'Can I afford this?' And if not in whole, how about in part? With such vital information in hand, you are now better able to design an appropriate acceleration program that fits your target in terms of the desired pay off date and the amount of monthly payment you should be able to afford in order to meet the desired payoff date. Basically, you'll check different payoff dates to get the particular amount of monthly payment you can feel comfortable with – the one you feel you can comfortably afford. And that (the affordability factor) should largely dictate the practicable and right payment amount or payoff date for you, or the speed at which you'll realistically be able to own your home debt-free and clear.

If you were to find, for example, that the $915.87 per month for a 20-year payoff date is too high within the limits of your monthly financial budget, you simply keep checking other repayment terms – say, a payoff date of 22 years, or of 25 years. A payoff date of 25 years, for example, will require a monthly payment of $856.39, meaning an additional amount of only $33.71 per month, down from $93.19 additional that you would have to pay for a 20 year payoff date.

And, finally, whatever payoff date you select, you still cannot view it as fixed, or as permanent and unchangeable. Rather, such a date must be viewed as strictly flexible and subject to modification based on future changes in your income and financial needs and obligations. You must be able to change your repayment plan as your financial circumstances evolve.

H. Keep A Constant Separate Track, Yourself, of Your Prepayments

If you are to truly derive the deserving rewards of, and the maximum benefits for, the sacrifices you've made in making the extra payments to make possible a more rapid elimination of your mortgage debt, there is one fundamental imperative that you must comply with, namely: you must, yourself, personally maintain a reliable and systematic way by which to police and keep a close track of all your payments. ***This is a MUST, absolutely non-negotiable.*** The danger is very real and not at all uncommon with lenders and banks, that you might make substantial payments and extra payments and, through some errors by the lenders, not receive the full credit for them. Consequently, to make absolutely sure that this would not happen with you, you've got to act as your own watchdog in your own behalf.

[See Chapter 9 for details on this, and for the basic tools for the track-keeping task]

---

[*] To calculate the payment you'll require at a given rate of interest (say 10%) and for a given number or of years (say 15 years), refer to the amortization table in the Appendix. Locate the column for the interest rate of your mortgage (say it's 10%). Then find the line for the number of years you'd like to pay off your loan (say 15 years). Multiply that factor by the present balance of your loan to get the monthly payment.

I. You Must Be Dedicated And Disciplined, And Stick To Your Prepayment Program Till The End

Finally, the critical key to the success of your mortgage payment acceleration program, is persistence and consistency in your acceleration plan. Indeed, experts contend that *probably the single most important but most widespread reason that most people who undertake prepayment programs ultimately fail, is that they don't remain consistent and persistent with the plan over the long haul.* They lack a clear long-term direction; they lack any sense of self-discipline. They don't stick to the original goal they set for themselves at the beginning—such as an original goal or promise, for example, to cut the life of a mortgage by 5 or 10 years, or to pay, say, an extra $25 or $50 each month towards their mortgage for a given number of years, or until the mortgage is fully paid off.

Yet, consistency and tough-minded, disciplined, dedication to the adopted accelerated payment plan of action on a sustained, long-term basis, is the essential ingredient without which even the best payment acceleration program cannot success. As Shaun Aghili, a widely respected author and expert of mortgage financing, very rightly put it, "Any prepayment strategy is only effective if done on a consistent and long-term basis. Unfortunately, the vast majority of people adopting this powerful strategy will abandon it within a few months or a year; way too early to reap any real benefit from it."[*]

In sum, if you are to undertake a successful payment acceleration program that will yield you all the stated great benefits of mortgage acceleration, you MUST be sure, first and foremost, to actually stick, without fail, with your prepayment plan, whatever its details or contents, for the very long haul. The rule of operation by which to ensure the occurrence of this, is simple but will always work if followed: just as you make it an obligation to pay your regular mortgage regularly each month (or for each month), make it your obligation, as well, with respect to your prepayment; whenever you send out your REGULAR month's payment each month, send out the EXTRA payment as well. Or, better still, simply view the total amount, both your regular payment and the prepayment extra, as your normal monthly mortgage payment with the same contractual obligation to pay all each and every single month—without fail or excuse whatsoever.

---

[*] *The No-Nonsense Credit Manual,* pp. 88-9

CHAPTER 11
REFINANCING YOUR MORTGAGE AS A SPECIAL TYPE OF MORTGAGE REDUCTION PLAN THAT CUTS DOWN YOUR INTEREST COSTS AS WELL

The principal subject matter of this manual is, of course, mortgage acceleration and the financial benefits that flow from it principally by way of reduction in interest costs. For the most part, the primary form of mortgage acceleration that is emphasized in this manual is mortgage prepayment. There is, however, yet another significant way of accelerating a homeowner's mortgage and cutting the interest costs, namely: ACCELERATION THROUGH THE REFINANCING OF ONE'S MORTGAGE.

In this chapter, we shall address such a strategy of mortgage acceleration through refinancing, and explore when it may be financially wise or advisable to undertake such a strategy and when it may not.

A. How Does Refinancing Work?

Whenever current interest rates turn lower than the rate homeowners are paying on their existing loan, it's not uncommon to find homeowners thinking in terms of "refinancing" – that is, taking out a new mortgage loan that has a lower rate of interest, and paying off the old mortgage that has the higher interest rate. The reason behind this attitude is simple: *a proper refinancing done at the right time and for the right margin of difference in interest rate, can be one of the best mortgage reduction moves a homeowner can make; a homeowner can certainly save and profit a great deal by having to pay a lower interest rate through replacing one loan with another.*

How, and in what ways, does having to pay a lower interest rate than what you've been paying benefit you as a homeowner? Essentially in three distinct ways: it can benefit you by reducing your monthly payment without changing the total interest cost you'll pay; it can benefit you by enabling you to pay off the loan in fewer years without changing the monthly payment; or it can benefit you by enabling you to pay off the loan for the same payment and in the same number of years but allow you to put more money in your pocket today.

In other words, refinancing could be a form of mortgage acceleration, and by some accounts, it could be one of the least painful methods of mortgage acceleration.

How big can the savings from a refinancing be for you?
Frankly, it can be quite large! Take this simple example.

EXAMPLE: Let's look at it here in terms of the potential savings in monthly payments. Let's suppose you had bought your home 5 years ago with a 30-year, $100,000 mortgage at 10 percent interest rate, and that now you want to refinance. Your monthly payments on the mortgage under these terms would be roughly $878, and after 5 years of payments your remaining balance on the loan would still be $96,574.

Now, let's say you refinance that mortgage with a new one under these terms: a new 30-year term at 7 percent. Your monthly payments on the $96,574 balance at the new, lower 7 percent rate, would be about $642, or $236 less (i.e., savings to you) each and every month—$878 minus $642. The savings of $236 each month ($878-$642) would mean a total of $70,800 in savings to you over the 25 years remaining until the original mortgage would be paid off. But, remember that in this example, the new loan is for a 30-year term, which means that since the time still remaining on the old, now-retired loan is 25 years, it will take an _additional_ 5 years to repay this new, 30-year loan. That is, for 5 years (60 months) you will still be paying the monthly rate ($642) on the new mortgage after the old mortgage would have been paid off. Calculating the cost of this, payment of $642 per month over a 5 year or 60 month period, comes to a total of $38,520. Hence, to get the total "net" savings you make from the refinancing deal, you subtract the additional $38,520 you'll have to pay because of the longer period of the new mortgage, from the $70,800 savings you make on the first mortgage on account of the reduced interest rate. Your net savings, then, in raw dollars from the refinancing deal comes to $32,280.

NOTE: It should be noted that, though your total savings in this example, in raw dollars, is $32,280, many economists and financial planners using the concept of the "time value of money" or the "present value" of money, would strongly argue that the true savings from this deal is even much larger because, it is said, you would also have been earning interest on the $236 per month that you would save over a period of many years (25 years in this example), although that interest accumulation is partially offset as you would as well forgo interest on $642 per month in the last 5 years. The theory, in a word, widely shared among economists and financial investors – and confirmed by common sense – can be summed up in one sentence: a $100 cash in your hand today is worth much more than $100 in your hand 25 years from now; for one thing, you could save or invest today the $100 at hand at, say, 5 percent annual interest and have $338.64 by the time the 25 year point rolls around.

Hence, using the concept of the "present value" of money to adjust for the interest accumulated based on the reasoning that you could invest your monthly savings at 5 percent interest, here's how the picture changes in the situation described above: you start with the fact that the savings you are making in lower interest payments, are $236 a month, or $2,832 a year. Invested at 5 percent interest (the rate of return) for 25 years, your interest-adjusted savings, on a compounded basis, would amount to $135,163. Now, you have to subtract from this the 5 years where you are losing $642 a month, or $7,704 a year; that's an interest adjusted amount in the sum of $42,569 that you have to take into account on the "expense" side. The direct dollar savings from the refinancing deal then is $135,163 minus $42,569, or a total of $92,594 – a figure that, as can be seen, is far, far larger than the $32,280 amount under the straight calculation method!

B. Factors To Consider In Deciding Whether To Refinance

To be sure, there's no doubt that a PRUDENT refinancing deal can be one of the wisest moves a homeowner can make. However, as you can probably imagine, the decision about refinancing – about whether at all to do it, in the first place, and when and under what conditions to do it – is not an easy decision at all. Why? Primarily because when you refinance, you have to incur a whole new array of closing and other costs. *Consequently, the most fundamental question to ask about refinancing, is not even "Can I get something by refinancing or how much can I get?" Rather, the real question is: "When is it best, when does it make sense to refinance, and under what conditions?"*

There are various factors that affect refinancing decision.

1. Interest Rate On Your Present Mortgage

This is often the triggering consideration with most people. In previous times, the then prevailing rule of thumb was that you'll need at least a 3-point differential before it will make economic sense to refinance, and that you should refinance your existing mortgage if interest rates dropped just three percentage points below the rate on your current mortgage. In more recent times, however, many experts now recommend that the homeowner may *consider* refinancing when the rate they can obtain is at least two percentage points below their existing rate.

This rule, though, is not absolute or automatic. In some cases it may pay to refinance even for less than the 2-point differential, while in other cases it may be ill-advised to refinance even to gain 3 percentage points or more. A major factor which will help determine which way to actually go, is the actual and accurate amount of the savings you expect to obtain through the lower monthly payments, and whether such savings will actually offset the considerable costs involved in refinancing a mortgage, and by how much. In deed, the answer to that central question will depend on the next important factor we'll consider which will affect your refinancing decision: namely, HOW LONG YOU WILL BE OCCUPYING THE HOME.

2. Length Of Time You Intend To Stay In The House

In any consideration of whether to refinance, one crucial factor is how long you expect to stay in the home at issue. And this is so for this simple reason: the costs of mortgage refinancing, as you will see below (see p. 81), are often considerable, and only if you can hold the house long enough, can you possibly recoup the costs of refinancing? If, for example, you plan to hold the property only for, say, three to five years, the closing costs will almost certainly swallow up the savings you stand to make from the refinancing, and in such a case you may have to seek a higher interest point differential, say 3 or 3.5 percentage points, to make refinancing economically viable and worthwhile. With a relatively long holding period, on the other hand, say 10 to 15 years, a 2-point interest differential may be sufficient to justify refinancing.

Indeed, financial experts advise that, ideally, when a homeowner who contemplates refinancing calculates what his "break-even point" on refinancing would be, it is not even sufficient for him to think just in terms of whether he'll be in the home at the break-even point or for a short time thereafter; but that he should be thinking in terms of for how long he's likely to stay AFTER the break-even point is reached. The central point is that, generally, the longer you will stay in the home, the more worthwhile a refinancing deal is (and vice versa), for it is only with such a longer period would you have been able to accumulate the years of interest savings sufficient to offset the refinancing costs.

3.   Your Current Financial Position

Another factor to consider when contemplating refinancing, is your current financial condition – your ability, TODAY, to meet the new mortgage requirements the lender will want in order for you to qualify for the refinanced mortgage amount you're seeking. ***Contrary to the common belief by the public, you should recognize that refinancing is essentially the same thing as going for a completely new loan.*** You are, in a word, seeking to obtain a new loan, another loan – but under different set of terms, particularly a different rate of interest. Hence, the new lender, even if he were to be the same lender holding your current mortgage, would require from you virtually all the usual qualifying requirements demanded of loan seekers: your credit history and record, including your record of payments on the current mortgage, your employment status, income level, outstanding debts, etc. In sum, *being certain that you can qualify for the refinanced loan, TODAY, just in the same way as you had qualified for the original loan years ago, is certainly a major factor you must consider when contemplating refinancing.*

C.   There Are Good Reasons, As Well As Bad Ones, For Which, And Situations When, Refinancing May Be Undertaken

To be sure, the 'bottom line' in refinancing, is to get more in interest savings over what you are to pay on your pre-existing mortgage, to get a better interest rate deal relative to the one you are paying on the pre-existing mortgage. Nevertheless, within the context of that common objective, there are a variety of reasons specific to individuals for which homeowners refinance their homes, some of which can be classified as "good" reasons and others as "bad." From the standpoint of sound financial planning, there are some reasons for which, and instances when, refinancing are deemed to make economic sense, and when they are not.

Some homeowners refinance to pay for a vacation, travel, a vacation home, or to purchase a new car, or to cover other personal expenses. Others refinance for the purpose of "consolidation" of their debts – basically taking the home equity you've built up over the years, which is supposedly "sitting idle" in the home, and using it to pay off various debts you owe, such as credit cards, store revolving account cards, personal loans, etc. And yet another common reason by some for refinancing is to free up some cash to pay for some needed expansion, improvement or repair work on the house.

Whatever your particular reason may be for wanting to refinance, probably the single most important thing to bear in mind in seeking refinancing, is this: that there are good and sound reasons for which you may refinance, as well a bad and unsound reasons; that there are instances and situations when refinancing perfectly makes good economic sense and are perfectly alright, and instances and situations when it does not and should not be undertaken.

How do you know when your motivation is a sound one and when it's not? It's rather simple. From the standpoint of prudent financial planning and wealth building, *in general when refinancing involves spending equity rather than preserving it, when the end result of refinancing means taking out your equity in the house and spending it, then watch out,* it's financially irresponsible and bad to refinance in such a situation because all you'll be doing in such a case is getting yourself into further debt that you'll still have to pay in the end. On the other hand, whenever you refinance to, in effect, convert your equity in the house from one form of equity to another form (as would be the case, for example, when you refinance to renovate your house), or when you refinance to increase equity in the house rather than to spend it, then that's when it's financially responsible and worthwhile refinancing. Refinancing your mortgage to use the proceeds to renovate and expand the home, for example, makes financial sense since the addition of, say, a bedroom or a garage to the property, or the expansion of your kitchen or living room, will increase the value of your house, and not take out your equity and spend it. But refinancing your mortgage so that you might free up enough cash to pay off consumer debts, such as for a vacation or to purchase a car, or to consolidate your debts, would be considered financially irresponsible and poor financial management since it spends and uses up equity you spent years to build, rather than preserving it.

Michael C. Thomsett, a noted financial planner, author and consultant, noting the ubiquitous televised ads by lending institutions which constantly encourage homeowners to refinance and take out loans on their 'idle home equity,' sums up quite clearly the general principle by which to properly differentiate between good reasons for refinancing and bad ones, this way:

> [Don't forget that] refinancing is the same thing as borrowing money. Lenders don't like to emphasize this, because they would rather have you think of refinancing as 'putting idle equity to work.' ... As a first step, think of refinancing as getting a new loan.
> A good rule of thumb, and one that will help you remain true to your own financial plan, is this: borrow money to increase equity, not spend it. Be a shrewd homeowner and investor by recognizing that equity is not the same thing as income .... equity is borrowing power, but it's also net worth. Depending on our financial goals, it could be more important to preserve equity than to pull it out and use it in some way....
> Assuming that you would like to own your home free and clear one-day, there must come a point where equity is allowed to build up undisturbed. That will mean not increasing your debt level in the future .... Remember what refinancing means: you'll have less equity to pull out and transfer later.

D.   The Costs Of Refinancing

As explained in Section A above, the savings that can be achieved from refinancing could be quite large. Unfortunately, it is not, however, that simple. It is not a one-way street: *refinancing is costly, as well*. Basically, the reason it's costly is because the actual procedure involved in refinancing is essentially the same as that involved in obtaining a completely brand new loan, and thus when you refinance you'll have to go through essentially the same steps and processes, the same expenditures and formalities that you went through when you originally bought the house, and you'll basically have to pay, again, most or almost all of the closing costs you paid when you bought the house initially.

How much in closing or other costs? Suffice it to say, simply, that it could be substantial. Experts estimate, for example, that closing costs for a home purchase often run 7 percent of the mortgage amount. Thus, using such estimate as a rough rule-of-thumb, the refinancing of a $100,000 mortgage amount should cost you roughly $7,000 in closing costs.

Here are a brief summary of some of the closing costs you will probably have to pay all over again in a refinancing:

1. *Points or Loan Origination Fee.* This is a fee imposed by the lender beyond the regular interest rate and paid in advance. One "point" equals one percent of the loan amount. Generally the biggest expense involved in refinancing, the points charges, will vary from one to three points, and even higher, depending upon various factors, such as the borrower's credit rating, loan-to-value ratio, whether property is owner-occupied or not, etc.

2. *Attorney's Fees.* Not only your own attorney's fees (if you use one), but in most cases your new lender's attorney's fees, as well.

3. *Title Insurance.* Your new lender will likely require you to obtain a new title insurance policy, just in case the title search misses some uncovered impairment to your ownership. Depending on the size of the loan, this may cost you anywhere from $300 - $1,000 in insurance premium.

4. *Title Check.* Your new lender will still want to be assured that you truly are the owner of the property. So, he will hire a title search agent to do the title checking, and you reimburse the lender for the cost of the agent's services.

5. *Credit Check.* The lender will run a credit check to check out your credit worthiness for which you'll be charged a small fee.

6. *Survey.* Your new lender may require that you obtain a new survey map, at a cost of roughly $100 to $400, especially if the previous survey is a very old one. A survey shows the exact legal description, boundaries and location of the property.

7. ***Escrow.*** There will be an escrow fee since refinancing will involve escrow just as the initial home purchase transaction did.

8. ***Appraisal Fee.*** The new lender may have to appraise the property to get its current appraised value, and for this it will usually use one of its own appraisers and charge you the cost of the appraisal fee.

9. ***Mortgage Tax.*** In those states that charge a mortgage tax for taking out a home mortgage, you may have to pay a state or county mortgage tax all over again since you're getting a new mortgage.

10. ***Prepayment Penalty.*** If such a penalty is stipulated in your old mortgage contract, your existing lender may impose a pre-payment penalty on you to retire your old mortgage. Such a penalty could be huge; it could be as high as 6 months worth of extra interest.

11. ***Other Costs.*** Other costs and charges which could be payable as a result of refinancing, include the following: document preparation fee chargeable by the escrow company for preparation of certain documents, document recording fees to record the necessary documents with the county records office, and termite inspection fees.

To sum it all up, the point of this exercise is simply this: to emphasize that the closing costs involved in refinancing is no ordinary matter and could be substantial. And the very important underlying reason for showing that such closing costs are substantial, is to make yet another point which is even more fundamental, namely, that *in doing refinancing, it is critically important that you first gather the facts and make as precise an estimate of the closing costs as possible; and that only then can you be in a position to make a prudent determination as to whether to refinance or not to.*

E. Should You Refinance?

As you can see from the preceding discussion, the process of refinancing involves far more than the question: 'How much can I get out of it?' As stated earlier in this chapter, the real question to ask about whether to refinance is actually, 'When does it make sense to do it?' And, by way of summarizing, we have largely concluded that refinancing might make financial sense only if the following conditions apply to you:

1. If you refinance for the right and proper reasons and plan to use the proceeds wisely; and if the purchases or investments you make with the proceeds are such that they will increase your net worth, such as by enabling a purchase of other assets that will grow in value, such as rental real estate.

2. If the Interest rates, as well as your new monthly payments, will in reality be lower.

3. If you will remain as owner of the house for a long duration, long enough to recoup the closing costs involved in the refinancing.

How do you figure your break-even point, which will indicate how long it will take to offset the cost of refinancing? There's a formula for it, which reads as follows:

Total refinancing cost	=	Number of months
Monthly savings		it takes to break even

First, estimate the total costs involved in refinancing. (Ask the lender to estimate this for you, since he's required under the truth-in-lending requirements to give you a good faith estimate of such costs, anyway.) Next, compare your present monthly payment to the monthly payment you'll need to make with the new mortgage. Then, divide the total refinancing cost by the savings in your monthly payment. The resultant figure equals your break-even point. Thus, assuming that your total refinancing costs are $3,000 and that by refinancing you will reduce your monthly payment by $80 per month, it will take about 38 months to absorb that cost, or to break even from this refinancing, as follows:

$$\frac{\$3,000}{\$80 \text{ per month}} = 37.5 \text{ months}$$

Thus, in the above example, if the homeowner plans to keep this house for more than 38 months, it will make financial sense for him to refinance. But it he plans to sell it (or can foresee selling it) within 38 months, it will not be a wise move to refinance.

4. The final condition when it will make financial sense to refinance, is if the final pay-off date remains the same or shortened. Financing will make sense when BOTH of these conditions equally obtain: the break-even test must work, and the repayment date is the same as on the original loan, or earlier, since any extension of the repayment term will mean additional interest costs (lesser savings) to you.

Thus, in a situation where and when the amount to be borrowed is higher than the current balance of the loan, or the repayment term is longer (say there are 20 years remaining on the original loan but the term will be extended to 30 years upon refinancing), you must adjust for these changes in your calculation in determining whether financing will make sense. Basically, to determine the break-even point on the comparable basis, you'll have to adjust the repayment level to what it would be if the term were the same. Request for assistance from your lender, he can help you make such a calculation. Also, you can use Appendix B to calculate what your payments would be.[*]

---

[*] For example, let's say you have an original 30-year mortgage that is refinanced when only 20 years is left on it but is refinanced for another 30-year term. What you'll do would be to tie it, instead, to the original pay off period – that is, calculate what the payments would have been if the repayment term were 20 years, instead. In the same manner, the process is the same if you borrow a refinanced amount that is higher than the existing balance: focus on what your payments would have been if you had borrowed the same refinanced amount as **the one you now owe**. For example, if your current balance on your original mortgage is $90,000, and that mortgage had been taken out 10 years ago in the amount of $100,000, and you are refinancing for (borrowing against) $100,000, you would make your calculations on $90,000.

F. Using The Refinancing Worksheet To Determine When Refinancing May Be Wise

The following worksheet (Table 11-1), reproduced for illustrative purposes from an informative Consumer Reports Books publication,[*] has been found by the present writer to be an excellent worksheet by which to work through the critical question of whether or not to refinance a mortgage, and when a refinancing move may make financial sense. Its great value lies in the step-by-step approach it provides for working through the essential calculations. With photocopies of the worksheets, necessary updates and revisions could be make in the calculations. To use the worksheet, you'll need to draw also from other data, such as those set forth in Tables 11-2 & 11-3 below.

Table 11-1. Mortgage Refinancing Worksheet: step-by-step calculations to aid in deciding on whether to replace your existing mortgage with a new one.

Mortgage Refinancing Worksheet

A. In what year will your current mortgage mature? _____

B. How many years is that date from now? _____ years

C. Enter your current monthly payment. $_____

D. Enter the term, in years, of the proposed new mortgage. _____ years

E. Enter your current monthly payment for principal and interest. (This is item C minus the portion of your monthly payment that goes into an escrow account to pay for taxes and/or insurance.) $_____

F. Enter the proposed monthly payment for principal and interest under the new mortgage. $_____

G. Subtract item F from item E to determine how much you would save per month if you refinance. $_____

H. Multiply monthly savings (item G) by 12 to get the annual savings. $_____

I. Multiply the annual savings (item H) by an interest factor from Table 11-2 on page 86). Use the factor for the number of years until your original mortgage expires (item B). $_____

---

[*] These three tables are reproduced from John R. Horfman, *"The Mortgage Book,"* *(Consumer Reports Books: New York, 1992)*, pp. 152-4, to whom the present writer and the publisher are deeply indebted and grateful.

Items J through O on this worksheet apply only if the old and new mortgages will mature at different times. If they will mature at the same time, skip straight to item P.

J. Will the new mortgage last longer than the old one? If so, by how many years? (If not, enter zero for items J, K, and L.) _____ years

K. Multiply monthly payment on the new mortgage (item F) by 12 to get annual payment on the new mortgage. $_____

L. Multiply the annual payment on the new mortgage (item K) by an interest factor from Table 11-2 on page 86). Use a factor for the number of years by which the new mortgage will outlast the old one (item J). $_____

M. Will the new mortgage mature sooner than the old one? If so, by how many years? (If it won't mature sooner, enter zero for items M, N, and O.) _____ years

N. Multiply the monthly payment on the old mortgage (item E) by 12 to get the annual payment on old mortgage. $_____

O. Multiply the annual payment on old mortgage (item N) by an interest factor from Table 11-2 on page 86). Use a factor for the number of years by which the new mortgage will mature sooner than the old one (item M). $_____

P. Enter your best estimate of the closing costs for refinancing your mortgage. If you have no estimate at this time, use 7 percent of the amount of the new mortgage. $_____

Q. Multiply your estimate of closing costs by an interest factor chosen from Table 11-3 on page 86). Choose a factor of either the number of years until your old mortgage matures, or 25 years, whichever is greater. $_____

Now you are ready to calculate your savings from refinancing.

R. Add items I and O, which represent the potential benefits (gross savings) to you from refinancing. $_____

S. From the gross savings total in item R, subtract items L and Q. They represent costs to you of refinancing. Enter the difference here. $_____

This is the savings to you from refinancing. The total amount is adjusted for interest you could earn at 5 percent if you did not spend this money on mortgage payments.

Generally, it is wise to refinance if the total in item S is at least $10,000 and at least triple the amount of the closing costs shown in item Q. Also, item H, the annual savings from refinancing, should normally be 25 percent or more of item Q, closing costs. That way, your payback period for breaking even on the refinancing is less than four years. If both of these conditions are met, you have a green light. Go ahead and refinance.

Table 11-2. Annual Interest Factors

This table shows the effect of saving or investing a given amount of money each year at 5 percent interest.

Number of Years	Interest Factor	Number of Years	Interest Factor
1	1.05	16	24.8
2	2.15	17	27.1
3	3.31	18	29.5
4	4.52	19	32.1
5	5.80	20	34.7
6	7.14	21	37.5
7	8.55	22	40.4
8	10.0	23	43.5
9	11.5	24	46.7
10	13.2	25	50.1
11	14.9	26	53.7
12	16.7	27	57.4
13	18.6	28	61.3
14	20.6	29	65.4
15	22.7		

Table 11-3. Long-term Interest Factors

This table shows the effect of saving or investing a lump sum of money at 5 percent interest over a certain number of years.

Number of Years	Interest Factor	Number of Years	Interest Factor
1	1.05	16	2.18
2	1.10	17	2.29
3	1.16	18	2.41
4	1.22	19	2.53
5	1.28	20	2.65
6	1.34	21	2.79
7	1.41	22	2.93
8	1.48	23	3.07
9	1.55	24	3.23
10	1.63	25	3.39
11	1.71	26	3.56
12	1.80	27	3.73
13	1.89	28	3.92
14	1.98	29	4.12
15	2.08		

Appendix A

SOME MODERN-DAY TYPES OF "CREATIVE FINANCING" MORTGAGES AND HOME FINANCING PLANS: A PRIMER

As already explained in several sections elsewhere in this manual (see especially p. 50), the vast majority of people who seek to buy a house cannot usually afford to personally finance the purchase, but must, of necessity, have to seek its financing through a mortgage loan. Consequently, the home mortgage industry is a key, pivotal integral part of the home buying and selling process for any interested party.

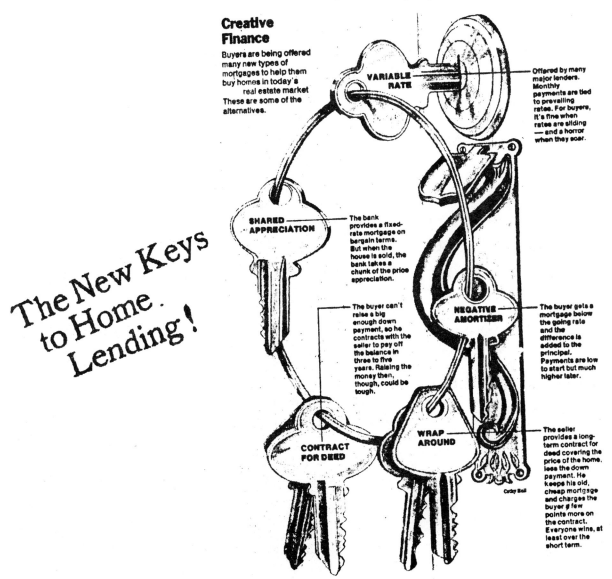

Creative Finance

Buyers are being offered many new types of mortgages to help them buy homes in today's real estate market. These are some of the alternatives.

The New Keys to Home Lending!

VARIABLE RATE — Offered by many major lenders. Monthly payments are tied to prevailing rates. For buyers, it's fine when rates are sliding — and a horror when they soar.

SHARED APPRECIATION — The bank provides a fixed-rate mortgage on bargain terms. But when the house is sold, the bank takes a chunk of the price appreciation.

NEGATIVE AMORTIZER — The buyer gets a mortgage below the going rate and the difference is added to the principal. Payments are low to start but much higher later.

CONTRACT FOR DEED — The buyer can't raise a big enough down payment, so he contracts with the seller to pay off the balance in three to five years. Raising the money then, though, could be tough.

WRAP AROUND — The seller provides a long-term contract for deed covering the price of the home, less the down payment. He keeps his old, cheap mortgage and charges the buyer a few points more on the contract. Everyone wins, at least over the short term.

Cathy Ball

In deed, by almost all accounts, home financing has become the single most overriding concern of the home buyer, seller, and real estate professional of the recent times, and the dominant determinant of whether or not a given home transfer deal is consummated.* As a rule, for the average home buyer, the search for the mortgage money would begin quite early in the game, directly after a home has been found and the contract signed, and continue indefinitely thereafter. In the process, the aspiring home buyer must necessarily go through the financial maze of the arcane world of the "mortgage industry," and while doing so, a whole range of questions must often be asked and decisions made, all of which will ultimately determine not only whether the aspiring home buyer succeeds in buying a house, but also whether he can do so under the best possible financial and legal terms. This, then, to our mind, makes it needful to devote a separate chapter on the basic facts and broad essentials, though by no means an exhaustive or even detailed exposition, of the modern-day mortgage world as they exist as of this writing.

Until recently, traditional mortgage features were a relatively uncomplicated and predictable matter—they generally had a fixed interest rate and a full amortization (or transfer of equity) over a relatively long and fixed period of 20 to 30 years. But, much of that has changed dramatically in recent times. Today, interest rates and purchase prices of homes have become dramatically fluctuating and unpredictable, or at least, potentially and prospectively so, resulting in the emergence of a whole new variety of mortgage plans—the so-called **"creative financing" mortgages.** SUCH RECENT DEVELOPMENT IS ONE FURTHER REASON WHY IT IS INCREASINGLY IMPERATIVE THAT THE HOME BUYER (AS WELL AS THE HOME SELLER) SUFFICIENTLY EDUCATE HIMSELF IN THE BASIC CONCEPTS AND TECHNIQUES OF MODERN HOME MORTGAGE FINANCING: *IT CAN SAVE YOU TIME AND MONEY; IT CAN PREVENT YOU FROM GETTING A MORTGAGE THAT IS ILL-SUITED TO YOUR NEEDS AND BEST INTERESTS; AND, ABOVE ALL, IT CAN MAKE THE DIFFERENCE BETWEEN YOUR ULTIMATELY BEING ABLE TO PURCHASE, AND TO KEEP, THAT DREAM HOUSE OR NOT BEING ABLE TO!*

A. What Is a Mortgage?

A mortgage is a loan contract; it's a special loan given especially for the purpose of buying real property. The term is also used to mean a lien on real property given by a homeowner or buyer (borrower) to his lender as security for the borrowed money.

Here's how it works. A lender agrees to provide you the money you need to buy a specific home or piece of real property. You, in turn, promise to repay the money based on terms set forth in the mortgage (loan) contract.

---

*Thomas L. Friedman of the New York Times, not long ago summed it up this way: "The costs and complications involved in financing a home in today's world of 19 percent mortgages have become so great that they are supplanting the house itself as the most important aspect of any purchase. People in America no longer shop for homes; they shop for financing...Financing has always been a serious concern in the selection of any home, but it has become the overriding concern now that most Americans can no longer qualify for the simple, low-cost, fixed-rate, 30-year bank mortgage that sustained their parents and grandparents since the 1930's." (N.Y. Times, Sunday, Oct. 4, 1983, Section 3, pp. 1 & 17, "The New Keys to Home Lending.")

Under the *Federal Truth in Lending Law,* the contract should state the amount of the loan, the annual percentage rate (which, when computed, includes the mortgage interest rate, the premium paid for insurance, the mortgage, and "discount points"), the size of the repayment, and the frequency of payments.

As a borrower, you pledge your home as security. It remains pledged until the loan is paid off. If you fail to meet the terms of the contract, the lender has the right to "foreclose", that is, obtain possession of the property, but he must follow the prescribed formalities of law to exercise the right of foreclosure.

Under the laws of most states in the East, the mortgagor (the borrower) retains title to the property, and the mortgage document does not give the mortgagee (the lender) title to the property, but merely gives him a lien (a claim) against the property. For most states west of the Mississippi, however, the mortgage arrangement is slightly different. Here, instead of the buyer receiving the actual title of ownership directly from the seller at the time of the purchase deal, a document is created, known as a *TRUST DEED* (also called *"Deed of Trust," "Mortgage Deed,"* or *"Deed to Secure Debt,"* depending on which state) for "holding the title during the mortgage period. This way, the power to carry out a foreclosure, should need be, is, in effect, vested in a third party and thereby makes it even easier for the lender to force a sale of the property if the borrower defaults on his mortgage payments as the lender would not have to go through many of the legal formalities and complications involved in formal foreclosures. In such western and other states (Alabama, Arkansas, Connecticut, Illinois, Maine, Maryland, Massachusetts, Missouri, New Hampshire, New Jersey, North Carolina, Ohio, Pennsylvania, Rhode Island, Tennessee, Vermont, and W. Virginia), the mortgage is, in fact, the deed, and the lender is legally regarded as the virtual owner of the property—until the mortgage loan has been repaid.

B. Some Major Financing Plans in Today's Market*

Given below, are some 13 home financing plans and techniques, representing the more basic variants of "creative home financing" on the market as of this writing. It's not attempted to outline every new or currently existing financing technique on the market since new financing alternatives are frequently being introduced while many of the existing ones frequently grow obsolete or disappear from the scene just as fast.

1. Fixed Rate Mortgage

Fixed rate mortgage is one having an interest rate and monthly payments that remain constant over the life of the loan. For example, suppose you borrow $50,000 at 10% interest for 30 years. Your monthly payments on this loan would be $632.22 and will never exceed that fixed predetermined amount.

Under the current market conditions, fixed rate mortgages are no more as readily available as they once were in the years past. Many lenders are reluctant to grant such mortgages nowadays, as they fear that a fixed rate would, in effect, lock them in a rate structure and they would not be able to adapt to new conditions in a market that is changeable.

2. Flexible Rate Mortgage

Flexible Rate Mortgage (also called "rollover," "adjustable," "variable" interest mortgage) is a mortgage with an interest rate which increases or decreases over the period of the loan according to pre-determined market conditions. The interest rate (the "price" of the loan) is not fixed, but is recomputed from time to time according to a certain financial index. One financial index commonly used, is the so-called "prime rate", the rate banks charge their most creditworthy customers to lend them money. However, the mortgage rate could be tied to one of the other financial indices less frequently used —e.g. , say the 3 to 5 year U.S. Treasury bill rate, or the Federal Home Loan Bank Board's interest rate, or some other price index.

The object for which the lender desires flexible-rate type of mortgages, is to protect himself against inflation and higher interest rates for his money, as he will be constantly able to keep his mortgage charges up as the market rates change (upwards) from time to time.

---

*Much of the rest of this appendix is excerpted from "The Mortgage Money Guide," an excellent booklet prepared and published under the auspices of the Federal Trade Commission by its staff members as a public service to home buyers. The present author is indebted to the FTC and its staff for this material.

There are many *variations* within the flexible-rate mortgage category.

To build predictability into your flexible rate loan, some lenders include provisions for "caps" that limit the amount your interest rate may change—a so-called "rate cap". Then, there is the "periodic cap", which

Rollover Mortgages: An Example

Tables show mortgage rates and monthly payments on a $75,000, 30-year rollover mortgage with an initial rate of 12.5 percent that is renegotiated (or "rolled over") every three years. The rate may rise or fall by a maximum of 5 percentage points over the life of the mortgage, and that the rate can fluctuate by no more than 1.5 percentage points during each renegotiation. Assume the rate rises or falls by the maximum allowed at each renegotiation.

If Rates Go UP:	MORTGAGE RATE	MONTHLY PAYMENT	If Rates Go DOWN:	MORTGAGE RATE	MONTHLY PAYMENT
Year 1	12.5%	$ 800.44	Year 1	12.5%	$800.44
Year 4	14.0%	$ 885.95	Year 4	11.0%	$717.16
Year 7	15.5%	$ 970.21	Year 7	9.5%	$640.76
Year 10	17.0%	$1,052.57	Year 10	8.0%	$573.01
Year 13	17.5%	$1,078.92	Year 13	7.5%	$553.37

Source: Federal Home Loan Bank Board

The New York Times/May 31, 1980

limits the amount the rate can increase at any one time [for example, a provision in the mortgage that even if the index increases by 2% in one year, the borrower's rate can only go up 1%]; and there's the "aggregate cap", which limits the amount the rate can increase over the life of the loan [e.g., a provision that even if the index increases by, say 2% every year, the borrower's rate cannot increase more than 5% over the life of the loan.]

Another variation of the flexible-rate mortgage is to fix the interest rate for a period of time— 3 to 5 years, for example — with the understanding that the interest rate will then be renegotiated. Loans with periodically renegotiated rates are also called *rollover mortgages;* and because the interest rate is fixed for at least a reasonable length of time, such loans make monthly payments more predictable. And, a final variation of the flexible rate mortgage we shall take note of here, is the *pledged account buy-down mortgage* with a flexible rate. Under this plan, the buyer (or it could be the builder, or anyone else willing to subsidize the loan) makes a large initial payment to the lender at the time the loan is made. The payment is placed in an interest-earning account with the lender, thereby offsetting the mortgage rate you pay and helping lower your interest rate for at least the first few years.

3. Balloon Mortgage

A balloon mortgage is one in which only the interest due is paid during the term of the mortgage, with the entire loan principal due and payable at the end of the term (which is usually a short one, commonly 3 to 5 years). Notwithstanding that the equal monthly payments to be paid in balloon mortgage plans are for the interest charge only, nevertheless that interest rate is a fixed rate thoughout the life of the loan.

Here's how a typical balloon plan works. Suppose you borrow $30,000 for a 5 year term at a 15% interest rate. And suppose your payments per month are only $375. In this example, payments of $375 per month for a 5-year period only amounts to a sum just equal to the interest charge on the loan, which means that the $30,000 principal becomes due at maturity—at the end of the 5 year period. That means, in other words, that after you shall have made 59 monthly payments of $375 each, you will then have to make one final, big ("balloon") payment of $30,375. And what if you can't make that final payment? Then you'll have to refinance the property, if that is available, or sell the property.

Some (not all) lenders guarantee refinancing when the balloon payment is due, though no guarantee is usually made on the associated interest rate. When no such guarantee on refinancing exists, the borrower (home buyer) could be forced to start the whole business of shopping for housing money once again, as well as paying closing costs and front-end charges all over again.

4. Graduated Payment Mortgage

Graduated Payment Mortgages (GPM) are designed for home buyers who expect to be able to make larger monthly payments in the near future.   During the early years of the loan, the borrower makes lower monthly payments. The payments are structured to rise at a set rate over a set period, say 5 or 10 years. Then they remain constant for the remaining duration of the loan.

Even though the payments change, the interest rate is usually fixed. So, during the early years, the borrower's payments are lower than the amount that would have been warranted by the interest rate. During the later years, the difference is made up by higher payments.   At the end of the loan period, the borrower would have paid off his entire debt.

5. Growing Equity Mortgage (Rapid Payoff Mortgage)

The "Growing Equity Mortgage" (GEM) and the "Rapid Payoff Mortgage" are among the more recent of mortgage plans on the market. These mortgages combine a fixed interest rate with a changing monthly payment. The interest rate is usually a few percentage points below the market rate. Although the mortgage term may run for 30 years, the loan will frequently be paid off in less than 15 years because payment increases are applied entirely to the principal.

Monthly payment changes are based on agreed-upon schedule of increases or on an index. For example, the plan might use the U.S. Commerce Department index that measures after-tax per capita income, and your payments might increase at a specified portion of the change in this index, say 75%.

Suppose you're paying $500 per month. In this example, if the index increases by 8%, you will have to pay 75% of the 8%, i.e., 6%, additional. Your payment increase, then, is to $530, and the additional $30 you pay will be used to reduce your principal.

To be able to use this mortgage plan, you have to have an income that is rising rapidly enough to keep pace with the increased payments.   The chief advantage of this plan is that it can often permit the borrower to pay off his loan and acquire equity in the property rapidly.

6. Shared Appreciation Mortgage

In Shared Appreciation Mortgage (SAM), you make monthly payments at a relatively low interest rate. You also agree to share with the lender a sizable percentage (usually 30% to 50%) of whatever appreciation comes about in your house's value after a specified number of years, or when you sell or transfer the home.

The principal advantage of this plan to a borrower (which, it is to be recognized, comes about because of the shared appreciation feature), is that he gets to enjoy monthly payments which are lower than is available with many other regular plans. However, he's subject to some potential risks associated with the plan. For example, he may still be liable for the dollar amount of the property's appreciation even if he does not wish to sell the property at the agreed-upon date. Also, if property values do not increase as anticipated, the borrower may still be liable for an additional amount of interest agreed upon.

Here is how one variation of this idea, called *shared equity mortgage plans,* works, for an example. Let's suppose you've found a home for $100,000 in a neighborhood where property values are rising, and that the local bank is charging 18% on home mortgages. Assuming you paid $20,000 down and chose a 30-year mortgage term on the $80,000 balance, your monthly payments would have to be $1,205.67—which, let's say, you'd find to be about twice what you can afford. But, along comes a friend who offers to help. He offers to pay half of each monthly payment, or roughly $600, for 5 years. At the end of that time, you both assume the house will be worth at least $125,000. You can sell it, and your friend can recover the share of the monthly payments he had made to date (i.e., $36,000), plus half of the home's appreciation, or $12,500, for a total of $48,500 to him. Or, you can at the time pay your friend the same sum of money out of your pocket and gain increased equity in the house.

Shared appreciation and shared equity mortgages were inspired partly by rising interest rates and partly by the notion that housing values would continue to grow and grow over the foreseeable future. It should always be realized therefore, that if property values fall, or don't rise as high or rapidly as anticipated, these plans may not be as available or advisable.

7. Assumable Mortgage

An assumable mortgage is a mortgage that can be passed on to a new owner at the previous owner's interest rate. For example, suppose you're interested in a $75,000 home. You make a down payment of $25,000, and you still owe $50,000. The owner of the home has paid off $20,000 of a $30,000, 10% mortgage. You assume the present owner's old mortgage, which has $10,000 outstanding. You also make additional financing arrangements for the remaining $40,000, by, for example, borrowing that amount from a mortgage company at the prevailing market rate of 16%. Your overall interest rate is lower than the market rate because part of the money you owe is being repaid at 10%.

It should be noted that, as a practical matter, during periods of high rates, most lending institutions are reluctant to permit assumptions, preferring to write a new mortgage at the prevailing market rate. In such times this results in many lenders calling in the loans under *"due on sale"* clauses (see Appendix E). Because these clauses have increasingly been upheld in court, many mortgages are no longer legally assumable. Be especially careful, therefore, if you are considering a mortgage represented as "assumable." Read the contract carefully and consider having an expert or professional check to determine if the lender has the right to raise your rate in those mortgages.

8. Seller Take-back

This mortgage, provided by the seller, is frequently a *"second trust"* and is combined with an assumed mortgage. The second trust (or *"second mortgage"*) provides financing in addition to the first assumed mortgage, using the same property as collateral. (In the event of default, the second mortgage is satisfied only after the first). Seller take-backs frequently involve payments for interest only, with the principal due at maturity.

For example, suppose you want to buy a $150,000 home, that the seller owes $70,000 on the house on a 10% mortgage, and that you assume this mortgage and make a $30,000 down payment. You still need $50,000. So the seller gives you a second mortgage, or take-back, for $50,000 for 5 years at 14% (well below the market rate) with payments of $583.33. However, your payments are for interest only, and in 5 years you will have to pay the $50,000 principal. The seller take-back, in other words, may have enabled you to buy the home. But it may also have left you with a sizable "balloon" payment that must be paid off in the near future.

Some private sellers are also offering first trusts as take-backs. In this approach, the seller finances the major portion of the loan and takes back a mortgage on the property.

9. Wraparound

Another variation on the second mortgage is the **wraparound**. Suppose you'd like to buy a $75,000 condominium and can make a $25,000 down payment, but can't afford the payments at the current rate (let's say it's 18%) on the remaining $50,000. The present owners have a $30,000, 10% mortgage. They offer you a $50,000 "wraparound" mortgage at 14%. The new loan "wraps around" the existing $30,000 mortgage, adding $20,000 to it. You make all your payments to the second lender or the seller, who then forwards payments for the first mortgage. You'll, in effect, be paying the equivalent of 10% on the $30,000 to the first lender, plus an additional 4% on this amount to the second lender, plus 14% on the remaining $20,000. Your total loan costs using this approach will be lower than if you obtained a loan for the full amount at the current rate (for example, 18%).

Wraparounds may cause problems if the original lender or the holder of the original mortgage is not aware of the new mortgage. Upon discovering this arrangement, some lenders or holders may have the right to insist that the old mortgage be paid off immediately.

10. Land Contract

Borrowed from commercial real estate, this plan enables you to pay below-market interest rates. The installment land contract permits the seller to hold onto his or her original below-market rate mortgage while "selling" the home on an installment basis. The installment payments are for a short term and may be for interest only. At the end of the contract the unpaid balance, frequently the full purchase price, must still be paid.

The seller continues to hold title to the property until all payments are made.   Thus, you, the buyer, acquire no equity until the contract ends. If you fail to make a payment on time, you could lose a major investment.

These loans are popular because they offer lower payments than market rate loans. Land contracts are also being used to avoid the ***due-on-sale clause*** (see Appendix E). The buyer and seller may assert to the lender who provided the original mortgage that the due on sale clause does not apply because the property will not be sold until the end of the contract. Therefore, the low interest rate continues. However, the lender may assert that the contract in fact represents a sale of the property. Consequently, the lender may have the right to accelerate the loan, or call it due, and raise the interest rate to current market levels.

11. Buy-down

A buy-down is a subsidy of the mortgage interest rate that helps you meet the payments during the first few years of the loan. Suppose a new house sells for $150,000, that after a down payment of $75,000, you still need to finance $75,000, and that a 30-year first mortgage is available for 17%, which would make your monthly payments $1,069.26, or beyond your budget. However, a buy-down is available: for the first three years, the developer will subsidize your payments, bringing down the interest rate to 14%. This means your payments are only $888.65, which you can afford.

There are several things to think about in buy-downs. First, consider what your payments will be after the first few years. If this is a fixed rate loan, the payments in the above example will jump to the rate at which the loan was originally made —17%—and total more than $1,000. If this is a flexible rate loan, and the index to which your rate is tied has risen since you took out the loan, your payments could go up even higher.

Second, check to see whether the subsidy is part of your contract with the lender or with the builder. If it's provided separately by the builder, the lender can still hold you liable for the full interest rate (17% in the above example), even if the builder backs out of the deal or goes out of business.

Finally, that $150,000 sales price may have been increased to cover the builder's interest subsidy. A comparable home may be selling around the corner for less. At the same time it may well be the case that competition encouraged the builder to offer you a genuine savings. It pays to check around.

There are also plans called ***consumer buy-downs.*** In these loans, the buyer makes a sizable down payment, and the interest rate granted is below market. In other words, in exchange for a large payment at the beginning of the loan, you may qualify for a lower rate on the amount borrowed. Frequently, this type of mortgage has a shorter term than those written at current market rates.

12. Rent With Option to Buy

In a climate of changing interest rates, some buyers and sellers are attracted to a ***rent-with-option*** arrangement. In this plan, you rent property and pay a premium for the right to purchase the property within a limited time period at a specific price. In some arrangements, you may apply part of the rental payments to the purchase price.

This approach enables you to lock in the purchase price. You can also use this method to "buy time" in the hope that interest rates will decrease. From the seller's perspective, this plan may provide the buyer time to obtain sufficient cash or acceptable financing to proceed with a purchase that may not be possible otherwise.

13. Zero Rate and Low Rate Mortgage

These mortgages are unique in that they appear to be completely or almost interest free.   The buyer makes a large down payment, usually one-third of the sales price, and pays the remainder in installments over a short term.

Suppose you want to buy a $90,000 home but you find the market interest rate unacceptable. You opt to use your savings to make the down payment, say $30,000, on a "zero rate" (or no-interest) mortgage.   Then you pay a front-end finance charge—for example, 12% of the money you need to borrow, or about $8,400.   You then agree to repay the principal ($60,000) in 84 monthly installments of $714.29. In 7 years, the loan will be paid off.

In these mortgages, the sales price may be increased to reflect the loan costs.   Thus, you could be exchanging lower interest costs for a higher purchase price.   Partly because of this, you may be able to deduct the prepaid finance charge and a percentage (for example, 10%) of your payments from your taxes as if it were interest.

14. Reverse Annuity Mortgage

If you already own your home and need to obtain cash, you might consider the reverse annuity mortgage (RAM) or *"equity conversion."*   In this plan, you obtain a loan in the form of monthly payments over an extended period of time, using your property as collateral.   When the loan comes due, you repay both the principal and interest.

A RAM is not a mortgage in the conventional sense. You can't obtain a RAM until you have paid off your original mortgage. Suppose you own your home and you need a source of money, you could draw up a contract with a lender that enables you to borrow a given amount each month until you've reached a maximum of, for example, $10,000. At the end of the term, you must repay the loan. But remember, if you do not have the cash available to repay the loan plus interest, you will have to sell the property or take out a new loan.

FIGURE A-1   HIGHLIGHTING THE ESSENTIALS OF CREATIVE FINANCING PLANS

Type	Description	Considerations
Fixed Rate Mortgage	Fixed interest rate, usually long-term; equal monthly payments of principal and interest until debt is paid in full.	Offers stability and long-term tax advantages; limited availability. Interest rates may be higher than other types of financing. New fixed rates are rarely assumable.
Flexible Rate Mortgage	Interest rate changes are based on a financial index, resulting in possible changes in your monthly payments, loan term, and/or principal. Some plans have rate or payment caps.	Readily available. Starting interest rate is slightly below market, but payments can increase sharply and frequently if index increases. Payment caps prevent wide fluctuations in payments but may cause negative amortization (see box, page 15). Rate caps, while rare, limit amount total debt can expand.
Renegotiable Rate Mortgage (Rollover)	Interest rate and monthly payments are constant for several years; changes possible thereafter. Long-term mortgage.	Less frequent changes in interest rate offer some stability.
Balloon Mortgage	Monthly payments based on fixed interest rate; usually short-term; payments may cover interest only with principal due in full at term end.	Offers low monthly payments but possibly no equity until loan is fully paid. When due, loan must be paid off or refinanced. Refinancing poses high risk rate mortgages.
Graduated Payment Mortgage	Lower monthly payments rise gradually (usually over 5-10 years), then level off for duration of term. With flexible interest rate, additional payment changes possible if index changes.	Easier to qualify for. Buyer's income must be able to keep pace with scheduled payment increases. With a flexible rate, payment increases beyond the graduated payments can result in additional negative amortization (see box, page 15).
Shared Appreciation Mortgage	Below-market interest rate and lower monthly payments, in exchange for a share of profits when property is sold or on a specified date. Many variations.	If home appreciates greatly, total cost of loan jumps. If home fails to appreciate, projected increase in value may still be due, requiring refinancing at possibly higher rates.
Assumable Mortgage	Buyer takes over seller's original, below-market rate mortgage.	Lowers monthly payments. May be prohibited if "due on sale" clause is in original mortgage (see box, page 12). Not permitted on most new fixed rate mortgages.
Seller Take-back	Seller provides all or part of financing with a first or second mortgage.	May offer a below-market interest rate; may have a balloon payment requiring full payment in a few years or refinancing at market rates, which could sharply increase debt.
Wraparound	Seller keeps original low rate mortgage. Buyer makes payments to seller who forwards a portion to the lender holding original mortgage. Offers lower effective interest rate on total transaction.	Lender may call in old mortgage and require higher rate. If buyer defaults, seller must take legal action to collect debt.
Growing Equity Mortgage (Rapid Payoff Mortgage)	Fixed interest rate but monthly payments may vary according to agreed-upon schedule or index.	Permits rapid payoff of debt because payment increases reduce principal. Buyer's income must be able to keep up with payment increases.
Land Contract	Seller retains original mortgage. No transfer of title until loan is fully paid. Equal monthly payments based on below-market interest rate with unpaid principal due at loan end.	May offer no equity until loan is fully paid. Buyer has few protections if conflict arises during loan.
Buy-down	Developer (or third party) provides an interest subsidy which lowers monthly payments during the first few years of the loan. Can have fixed or flexible interest rate.	Offers a break from higher payments during early years. Enables buyer with lower income to qualify. With flexible rate mortgage, payments may jump substantially at end of subsidy. Developer may increase selling price.
Rent with Option	Renter pays "option fee" for right to purchase property at specified time and agreed-upon price. Rent may or may not be applied to sales price.	Enables renter to buy time to obtain down payment and decide whether to purchase. Locks in price during inflationary times. Failure to take option means loss of option fee and rental payments.
Reverse Annuity Mortgage (Equity Conversion)	Borrower owns mortgage-free property and needs income. Lender makes monthly payments to borrower, using property as collateral.	Can provide homeowners with needed cash. At end of term, borrower must have money available to avoid selling property or refinancing.
Zero Rate and Low Rate Mortgage	Appears to be completely or almost interest free. Large down payment and one-time finance charge, then loan is repaid in fixed monthly payments over short term.	Permits quick ownership. May not lower total cost (because of possibly increased sales price). Doesn't offer long-term tax deductions.

APPENDIX B

APPENDIX B: (MORTGAGE) AMORTIZATION TABLES

How To Read The Tables In Appendix B

Appendix B tables show the monthly payments necessary to "amortize" (i.e., pay off) a loan at differing rates from 8 percent to 15 percent, and for amounts ranging from $50 to $100,000, and for terms of 5, 10, 15, 20, 25 and 30 years.

The formal steps and formulas by which you may figure out the principal, the interest, and the balances, even for other rates and amounts which are not specifically listed in the tables, are more elaborately outlined in Chapter 9, at pp. 64-69. However, note that, additionally, there are some few other simple, quick methods by which you may approximate, from the figures listed here, the monthly payments for other rates and amounts. For example, to estimate the payments for a loan at 9.125% interest, you may simply take the half-way point between 9 percent rate and 9.25 percent rate. For a mortgage of $81,000, you can multiply the $10,000 figure by 0.81. For $197,000 mortgage, you'll multiply the $100,000 figure by 1.97.

APPENDIX B: Amortization Tables: Monthly Payment Necessary To Amortize A Loan

8.50%

Amount	5 Years	10 Years	15 Years	20 Years	25 Years	30 Years
50	1.03	.62	.50	.44	.41	.39
100	2.06	1.24	.99	.87	.81	.77
500	10.26	6.20	4.93	4.34	4.03	3.85
1000	20.52	12.40	9.85	8.68	8.06	7.69
2000	41.04	24.80	19.70	17.36	16.11	15.38
5000	102.59	62.00	49.24	43.40	40.27	38.45
10000	205.17	123.99	98.48	86.79	80.53	76.90
15000	307.75	185.98	147.72	130.18	120.79	115.34
20000	410.34	247.98	196.95	173.57	161.05	153.79
25000	512.92	309.97	246.19	216.96	201.31	192.23
30000	615.50	371.96	295.43	260.35	241.57	230.68
35000	718.08	433.95	344.66	303.74	281.83	269.12
40000	820.67	495.95	393.90	347.13	322.10	307.57
45000	923.25	557.90	443.14	390.53	362.36	346.02
50000	1025.83	619.93	492.37	433.92	402.62	384.46
55000	1128.41	681.93	541.61	477.31	442.88	422.91
60000	1231.00	743.92	590.85	520.70	483.14	461.35
65000	1333.58	805.91	640.09	564.09	523.40	499.80
70000	1436.16	867.90	689.32	607.48	563.66	538.24
75000	1538.74	929.90	738.56	650.87	603.93	576.69
80000	1641.33	991.89	787.80	694.26	644.19	615.14
85000	1743.91	1053.88	837.03	737.65	684.45	653.58
90000	1846.49	1115.88	886.27	781.05	724.71	692.03
95000	1949.08	1177.87	935.51	824.44	764.97	730.47
100000	2051.66	1239.86	984.74	867.83	805.23	768.92

8.75%

Amount	5 Years	10 Years	15 Years	20 Years	25 Years	30 Years
50	1.04	.63	.50	.45	.42	.40
100	2.07	1.26	1.00	.89	.83	.79
500	10.32	6.27	5.00	4.42	4.12	3.94
1000	20.64	12.54	10.00	8.84	8.23	7.87
2000	41.28	25.07	19.99	17.68	16.45	15.74
5000	103.19	62.67	49.98	44.19	41.11	39.34
10000	206.38	125.33	99.95	88.38	82.22	78.68
15000	309.56	188.00	149.92	132.56	123.33	118.01
20000	412.75	250.66	199.89	176.75	164.43	157.35
25000	515.94	313.32	249.87	220.93	205.54	196.68
30000	619.12	375.99	299.84	265.12	246.65	236.02
35000	722.31	438.65	349.81	309.30	287.76	275.35
40000	825.49	501.31	399.78	353.49	328.86	314.69
45000	928.68	563.98	449.76	397.67	369.97	354.02
50000	1031.87	626.64	499.73	441.86	411.08	393.36
55000	1135.05	689.30	549.70	486.05	452.18	432.69
60000	1238.24	751.97	599.67	530.23	493.29	472.03
65000	1341.43	814.63	649.65	574.42	534.40	511.36
70000	1444.61	877.29	699.62	618.60	575.51	550.70
75000	1547.80	939.96	749.59	662.79	616.61	590.03
80000	1650.98	1002.62	799.56	706.97	657.72	629.37
85000	1754.17	1065.28	849.54	751.16	698.83	668.70
90000	1857.36	1127.95	899.51	795.34	739.93	708.04
95000	1960.54	1190.61	949.48	839.53	781.04	747.37
100000	2063.73	1253.27	999.45	883.72	822.15	786.71

8.00%

Amount	5 Years	10 Years	15 Years	20 Years	25 Years	30 Years
50	1.02	.61	.48	.42	.39	.37
100	2.03	1.22	.96	.84	.78	.74
500	10.14	6.07	4.78	4.19	3.86	3.67
1000	20.28	12.14	9.56	8.37	7.72	7.34
2000	40.56	24.27	19.12	16.73	15.44	14.68
5000	101.39	60.67	47.79	41.83	38.60	36.69
10000	202.77	121.33	95.57	83.65	77.19	73.38
15000	304.15	182.00	143.35	125.47	115.78	110.07
20000	405.53	242.66	191.14	167.29	154.37	146.76
25000	506.91	303.32	238.92	209.12	192.96	183.45
30000	608.30	363.99	286.70	250.94	231.55	220.13
35000	709.68	424.65	334.48	292.76	270.14	256.82
40000	811.06	485.32	382.27	334.58	308.73	293.51
45000	912.44	545.98	430.05	376.40	347.32	330.20
50000	1013.82	606.64	477.83	418.23	385.91	366.89
55000	1115.21	667.31	525.61	460.05	424.50	403.58
60000	1216.59	727.97	573.40	501.87	463.09	440.26
65000	1317.97	788.63	621.18	543.69	501.69	476.95
70000	1419.35	849.30	668.96	585.51	540.28	513.64
75000	1520.73	909.96	716.74	627.34	578.87	550.33
80000	1622.12	970.63	764.53	669.16	617.46	587.02
85000	1723.50	1031.29	812.31	710.98	656.05	623.70
90000	1824.88	1091.95	860.09	752.80	694.64	660.39
95000	1926.26	1152.62	907.87	794.62	733.23	697.08
100000	2027.64	1213.28	955.66	836.45	771.82	733.77

8.25%

Amount	5 Years	10 Years	15 Years	20 Years	25 Years	30 Years
50	1.02	.62	.49	.43	.40	.38
100	2.04	1.23	.98	.86	.79	.76
500	10.20	6.14	4.86	4.27	3.95	3.76
1000	20.40	12.27	9.71	8.53	7.89	7.52
2000	40.80	24.54	19.41	17.05	15.77	15.03
5000	101.99	61.33	48.51	42.61	39.43	37.57
10000	203.97	122.66	97.02	85.21	78.85	75.13
15000	305.95	183.98	145.53	127.81	118.27	112.69
20000	407.93	245.31	194.03	170.42	157.70	150.26
25000	509.91	306.64	242.54	213.02	197.12	187.82
30000	611.89	367.96	291.05	255.62	236.54	225.38
35000	713.87	429.29	339.55	298.23	275.96	262.95
40000	815.86	490.62	388.06	340.83	315.39	300.51
45000	917.84	551.94	436.57	383.43	354.81	338.07
50000	1019.82	613.27	485.08	426.04	394.23	375.64
55000	1121.80	674.59	533.58	468.64	433.65	413.20
60000	1223.78	735.92	582.09	511.24	473.08	450.76
65000	1325.74	797.25	630.60	553.85	512.50	488.33
70000	1427.74	858.57	679.10	596.45	551.92	525.89
75000	1529.72	919.90	727.61	639.05	591.34	563.45
80000	1631.71	981.23	776.12	681.66	630.77	601.02
85000	1733.69	1042.55	824.62	724.26	670.19	638.58
90000	1835.67	1103.88	873.13	766.86	709.61	676.14
95000	1937.65	1165.20	921.64	809.47	749.03	713.71
100000	2039.63	1226.53	970.15	852.07	788.46	751.27

9.50%

Amount	5 Years	10 Years	15 Years	20 Years	25 Years	30 Years
50	1.06	.65	.53	.47	.44	.43
100	2.11	1.30	1.05	.94	.88	.85
500	10.51	6.47	5.23	4.67	4.37	4.21
1000	21.01	12.94	10.45	9.33	8.74	8.41
2000	42.01	25.88	20.89	18.65	17.48	16.82
5000	105.01	64.70	52.22	46.61	43.69	42.05
10000	210.02	129.40	104.43	93.22	87.37	84.09
15000	315.03	194.10	156.64	139.82	131.06	126.13
20000	420.04	258.80	208.85	186.43	174.74	168.18
25000	525.05	323.50	261.06	233.04	218.43	210.22
30000	630.06	388.20	313.27	279.64	262.11	252.26
35000	735.07	452.90	365.48	326.25	305.80	294.30
40000	840.08	517.60	417.69	372.86	349.48	336.35
45000	945.09	582.29	469.91	419.46	393.17	378.39
50000	1050.10	646.99	522.12	466.07	436.85	420.43
55000	1155.11	711.69	574.33	512.68	480.54	462.47
60000	1260.12	776.39	626.54	559.28	524.22	504.52
65000	1365.13	841.09	678.75	605.89	567.91	546.56
70000	1470.14	905.79	730.96	652.50	611.59	588.60
75000	1575.14	970.49	783.17	699.10	655.28	630.65
80000	1680.15	1035.19	835.38	745.71	698.96	672.69
85000	1785.16	1099.88	887.60	792.32	742.65	714.73
90000	1890.17	1164.58	939.81	838.92	786.33	756.77
95000	1995.18	1229.28	992.02	885.53	830.02	798.82
100000	2100.19	1293.98	1044.23	932.14	873.70	840.86

9.75%

Amount	5 Years	10 Years	15 Years	20 Years	25 Years	30 Years
50	1.06	.66	.53	.48	.45	.43
100	2.12	1.31	1.06	.95	.90	.86
500	10.57	6.54	5.30	4.75	4.46	4.30
1000	21.13	13.08	10.60	9.49	8.92	8.60
2000	42.25	26.16	21.19	18.98	17.83	17.19
5000	105.63	65.39	52.97	47.43	44.56	42.96
10000	211.25	130.78	105.94	94.86	89.12	85.92
15000	316.87	196.16	158.91	142.28	133.68	128.88
20000	422.49	261.55	211.88	189.71	178.23	171.84
25000	528.11	326.93	264.85	237.13	222.79	214.79
30000	633.73	392.32	317.81	284.56	267.35	257.75
35000	739.35	457.70	370.78	331.99	311.90	300.71
40000	844.97	523.08	423.75	379.41	356.46	343.67
45000	950.60	588.47	476.72	426.84	401.02	386.62
50000	1056.22	653.86	529.69	474.26	445.57	429.58
55000	1161.84	719.24	582.65	521.69	490.13	472.54
60000	1267.46	784.63	635.62	569.12	534.69	515.50
65000	1373.08	850.01	688.59	616.54	579.24	558.46
70000	1478.70	915.40	741.56	663.97	623.80	601.41
75000	1584.32	980.78	794.53	711.39	668.36	644.37
80000	1689.94	1046.17	847.50	758.82	712.91	687.33
85000	1795.57	1111.55	900.46	806.24	757.47	730.29
90000	1901.19	1176.94	953.43	853.67	802.03	773.24
95000	2006.81	1242.32	1006.40	901.10	846.59	816.20
100000	2112.43	1307.71	1059.37	948.52	891.14	859.16

9.00%

Amount	5 Years	10 Years	15 Years	20 Years	25 Years	30 Years
50	1.04	.64	.51	.45	.42	.41
100	2.08	1.27	1.02	.90	.84	.81
500	10.38	6.34	5.08	4.50	4.20	4.03
1000	20.76	12.67	10.15	9.00	8.40	8.05
2000	41.52	25.34	20.29	18.00	16.79	16.10
5000	103.80	63.34	50.72	44.99	41.96	40.24
10000	207.59	126.68	101.43	89.98	83.92	80.47
15000	311.38	190.02	152.14	134.96	125.88	120.70
20000	415.17	253.36	202.86	179.95	167.84	160.93
25000	518.96	316.69	253.57	224.94	209.80	201.16
30000	622.76	380.03	304.28	269.92	251.76	241.39
35000	726.55	443.37	355.00	314.91	293.72	281.62
40000	830.34	506.71	405.71	359.90	335.68	321.85
45000	934.13	570.05	456.42	404.88	377.64	362.09
50000	1037.92	633.38	507.14	449.87	419.60	402.32
55000	1141.71	696.72	557.85	494.85	461.56	442.55
60000	1245.51	760.06	608.56	539.84	503.52	482.78
65000	1349.30	823.40	659.28	584.83	545.48	523.01
70000	1453.09	886.74	709.99	629.81	587.44	563.24
75000	1556.88	950.07	760.70	674.80	629.40	603.47
80000	1660.67	1013.41	811.42	719.79	671.36	643.70
85000	1764.47	1076.75	862.13	764.77	713.32	683.93
90000	1868.26	1140.09	912.84	809.76	755.28	724.17
95000	1972.05	1203.42	963.56	854.74	797.24	764.40
100000	2075.84	1266.76	1014.27	899.73	839.20	804.63

9.25%

Amount	5 Years	10 Years	15 Years	20 Years	25 Years	30 Years
50	1.05	.65	.52	.46	.43	.42
100	2.09	1.29	1.03	.92	.86	.83
500	10.44	6.41	5.15	4.58	4.29	4.12
1000	20.88	12.81	10.30	9.16	8.57	8.23
2000	41.76	25.61	20.59	18.32	17.13	16.46
5000	104.40	64.02	51.46	45.80	42.82	41.14
10000	208.80	128.04	102.92	91.59	85.64	82.27
15000	313.20	192.05	154.38	137.39	128.46	123.41
20000	417.60	256.07	205.84	183.18	171.28	164.54
25000	522.00	320.09	257.30	228.97	214.10	205.67
30000	626.40	384.10	308.76	274.77	256.92	246.81
35000	730.80	448.12	360.22	320.56	299.74	287.94
40000	835.20	512.14	411.68	366.35	342.56	329.08
45000	939.60	576.15	463.14	412.15	385.38	370.21
50000	1044.00	640.17	514.60	457.94	428.20	411.34
55000	1148.40	704.18	566.06	503.73	471.02	452.48
60000	1252.80	768.20	617.52	549.53	513.83	493.61
65000	1357.20	832.22	668.98	595.32	556.65	534.74
70000	1461.60	896.23	720.44	641.11	599.47	575.88
75000	1566.00	960.25	771.90	686.91	642.29	617.01
80000	1670.40	1024.27	823.36	732.70	685.11	658.15
85000	1774.80	1088.28	874.82	778.49	727.93	699.28
90000	1879.20	1152.30	926.28	824.29	770.75	740.41
95000	1983.60	1216.32	977.74	870.08	813.56	781.55
100000	2087.99	1280.33	1029.20	915.87	856.39	822.68

APPENDIX B: Amortization Tables: Monthly Payment Necessary To Amortize A Loan

10.00%

Amount	5 Years	10 Years	15 Years	20 Years	25 Years	30 Years
50	1.07	.67	.54	.49	.46	.44
100	2.13	1.33	1.08	.97	.91	.88
500	10.63	6.61	5.38	4.83	4.55	4.39
1000	21.25	13.22	10.75	9.66	9.09	8.78
2000	42.50	26.44	21.50	19.31	18.18	17.56
5000	106.24	66.08	53.74	48.26	45.44	43.88
10000	212.48	132.16	107.47	96.51	90.88	87.76
15000	318.71	198.23	161.20	144.76	136.31	131.64
20000	424.95	264.31	214.93	193.01	181.75	175.52
25000	531.18	330.38	268.66	241.26	227.18	219.40
30000	637.42	396.46	322.39	289.51	272.62	263.28
35000	743.65	462.53	376.12	337.76	318.05	307.16
40000	849.89	528.61	429.85	386.01	363.49	351.03
45000	956.12	594.68	483.58	434.26	408.92	394.91
50000	1062.36	660.76	537.31	482.52	454.36	438.79
55000	1168.59	726.83	591.04	530.77	499.79	482.67
60000	1274.83	792.91	644.77	579.02	545.23	526.55
65000	1381.06	858.98	698.50	627.27	590.66	570.43
70000	1487.30	925.06	752.23	675.52	636.10	614.31
75000	1593.53	991.14	805.96	723.77	681.53	658.18
80000	1699.77	1057.21	859.69	772.02	726.97	702.06
85000	1806.00	1123.29	913.42	820.27	772.40	745.94
90000	1912.24	1189.36	967.15	868.52	817.84	789.82
95000	2018.47	1255.44	1020.88	916.78	863.27	833.70
100000	2124.71	1321.51	1074.61	965.03	908.71	877.58

10.25%

Amount	5 Years	10 Years	15 Years	20 Years	25 Years	30 Years
50	1.07	.67	.55	.50	.47	.45
100	2.14	1.34	1.09	.99	.93	.90
500	10.69	6.68	5.45	4.91	4.64	4.49
1000	21.38	13.36	10.90	9.82	9.27	8.97
2000	42.75	26.71	21.80	19.64	18.53	17.93
5000	106.86	66.77	54.50	49.09	46.32	44.81
10000	213.71	133.54	109.00	98.17	92.64	89.62
15000	320.56	200.31	163.50	147.25	138.96	134.42
20000	427.41	267.08	218.00	196.33	185.28	179.23
25000	534.26	333.85	272.49	245.42	231.60	224.03
30000	641.11	400.62	326.99	294.50	277.92	268.84
35000	747.96	467.39	381.49	343.58	324.24	313.64
40000	854.82	534.16	435.99	392.66	370.56	358.45
45000	961.67	600.93	490.48	441.74	416.88	403.25
50000	1068.52	667.70	544.98	490.83	463.20	448.06
55000	1175.37	734.47	599.48	539.91	509.52	492.86
60000	1282.22	801.24	653.98	588.99	555.83	537.67
65000	1389.07	868.01	708.47	638.07	602.15	582.47
70000	1495.92	934.78	762.97	687.16	648.47	627.28
75000	1602.77	1001.55	817.47	736.24	694.79	672.08
80000	1709.63	1068.32	871.97	785.32	741.11	716.89
85000	1816.48	1135.09	926.46	834.40	787.43	761.69
90000	1923.33	1201.86	980.96	883.48	833.75	806.50
95000	2030.18	1268.63	1035.46	932.57	880.07	851.30
100000	2137.03	1335.40	1089.96	981.65	926.39	896.11

10.50%

Amount	5 Years	10 Years	15 Years	20 Years	25 Years	30 Years
50	1.08	.68	.56	.50	.48	.46
100	2.15	1.35	1.11	1.00	.95	.92
500	10.75	6.75	5.53	5.00	4.73	4.58
1000	21.50	13.50	11.06	9.99	9.45	9.15
2000	42.99	26.99	22.11	19.97	18.89	18.30
5000	107.47	67.47	55.27	49.92	47.21	45.74
10000	214.94	134.94	110.54	99.84	94.42	91.48
15000	322.41	202.41	165.81	149.76	141.63	137.22
20000	429.88	269.87	221.08	199.68	188.84	182.95
25000	537.35	337.34	276.35	249.60	236.05	228.69
30000	644.82	404.81	331.62	299.52	283.26	274.43
35000	752.29	472.28	386.89	349.44	330.47	320.16
40000	859.76	539.74	442.16	399.36	377.68	365.90
45000	967.23	607.21	497.43	449.28	424.89	411.64
50000	1074.70	674.68	552.70	499.19	472.10	457.37
55000	1182.17	742.15	607.97	549.11	519.30	503.11
60000	1289.64	809.61	663.24	599.03	566.51	548.85
65000	1397.11	877.08	718.51	648.95	613.72	594.59
70000	1504.58	944.55	773.78	698.87	660.93	640.32
75000	1612.05	1012.02	829.05	748.79	708.14	686.06
80000	1719.52	1079.49	884.32	798.71	755.35	731.80
85000	1826.99	1146.95	939.59	848.63	802.56	777.53
90000	1934.46	1214.42	994.86	898.55	849.77	823.27
95000	2041.93	1281.89	1050.13	948.47	896.98	869.01
100000	2149.40	1349.36	1105.40	998.38	944.19	914.74

10.75%

Amount	5 Years	10 Years	15 Years	20 Years	25 Years	30 Years
50	1.09	.69	.57	.51	.49	.47
100	2.17	1.37	1.13	1.02	.97	.94
500	10.81	6.82	5.61	5.08	4.82	4.67
1000	21.62	13.64	11.21	10.16	9.63	9.34
2000	43.24	27.27	22.42	20.31	19.25	18.67
5000	108.09	68.17	56.05	50.77	48.11	46.68
10000	216.18	136.34	112.10	101.53	96.21	93.35
15000	324.27	204.51	168.15	152.29	144.32	140.03
20000	432.36	272.68	224.20	203.05	192.42	186.70
25000	540.45	340.85	280.24	253.81	240.53	233.38
30000	648.54	409.02	336.29	304.57	288.63	280.05
35000	756.63	477.19	392.34	355.34	336.74	326.72
40000	864.72	545.36	448.38	406.10	384.84	373.40
45000	972.81	613.53	504.43	456.86	432.95	420.07
50000	1080.90	681.70	560.48	507.62	481.05	466.75
55000	1188.99	749.87	616.53	558.38	529.16	513.42
60000	1297.08	818.04	672.57	609.14	577.26	560.09
65000	1405.17	886.21	728.62	659.90	625.37	606.77
70000	1513.26	954.38	784.67	710.67	673.47	653.44
75000	1621.35	1022.55	840.72	761.43	721.57	700.12
80000	1729.44	1090.71	896.76	812.19	769.68	746.79
85000	1837.53	1158.88	952.81	862.95	817.78	793.46
90000	1945.62	1227.05	1008.86	913.71	865.89	840.14
95000	2053.71	1295.22	1064.91	964.47	913.99	886.81
100000	2161.80	1363.39	1120.95	1015.23	962.10	933.48

11.50%

Amount	5 Years	10 Years	15 Years	20 Years	25 Years	30 Years
50	1.10	.71	.59	.54	.51	.50
100	2.20	1.41	1.17	1.07	1.02	1.00
500	11.00	7.03	5.85	5.34	5.09	4.96
1000	22.00	14.06	11.69	10.67	10.17	9.91
2000	43.99	28.12	23.37	21.33	20.33	19.81
5000	109.97	70.30	58.41	53.33	50.83	49.52
10000	219.93	140.60	116.82	106.65	101.65	99.03
15000	329.89	210.90	175.23	159.97	152.48	148.55
20000	439.86	281.20	233.64	213.29	203.30	198.06
25000	549.82	351.49	292.05	266.61	254.12	247.58
30000	659.78	421.79	350.46	319.93	304.95	297.09
35000	769.71	492.09	408.87	373.26	355.77	346.61
40000	879.71	562.39	467.28	426.58	406.59	396.12
45000	989.67	632.68	525.69	479.90	457.42	445.64
50000	1099.64	702.98	584.10	533.22	508.24	495.15
55000	1209.60	773.28	642.51	586.54	559.06	544.67
60000	1319.56	843.58	700.92	639.86	609.89	594.18
65000	1429.52	913.88	759.33	693.18	660.71	643.69
70000	1539.49	984.17	817.74	746.51	711.53	693.21
75000	1649.45	1054.47	876.15	799.83	762.36	742.72
80000	1759.41	1124.77	934.56	853.15	813.18	792.24
85000	1869.38	1195.07	992.97	906.47	864.00	841.75
90000	1979.34	1265.36	1051.38	959.79	914.83	891.27
95000	2089.30	1335.66	1109.79	1013.11	965.65	940.78
100000	2199.27	1405.96	1168.19	1066.43	1016.47	990.30

11.75%

Amount	5 Years	10 Years	15 Years	20 Years	25 Years	30 Years
50	1.11	.72	.60	.55	.52	.51
100	2.22	1.43	1.19	1.09	1.04	1.01
500	11.06	7.11	5.93	5.42	5.18	5.05
1000	22.12	14.21	11.85	10.84	10.35	10.10
2000	44.24	28.41	23.69	21.68	20.70	20.19
5000	110.60	71.02	59.21	54.19	51.74	50.48
10000	221.19	142.03	118.42	108.38	103.48	100.95
15000	331.78	213.05	177.62	162.56	155.22	151.42
20000	442.37	284.06	236.83	216.75	206.96	201.89
25000	552.96	355.08	296.04	270.93	258.70	252.36
30000	663.55	426.09	355.24	325.12	310.44	302.83
35000	774.15	497.11	414.45	379.30	362.18	353.30
40000	884.74	568.12	473.66	433.49	413.92	403.77
45000	995.33	639.14	532.86	487.67	465.66	454.24
50000	1105.92	710.15	592.07	541.86	517.40	504.71
55000	1216.51	781.17	651.28	596.04	569.14	555.18
60000	1327.10	852.18	710.48	650.23	620.88	605.65
65000	1437.70	923.20	769.69	704.41	672.62	656.12
70000	1548.29	994.21	828.90	758.60	724.36	706.59
75000	1658.88	1065.23	888.10	812.79	776.10	757.06
80000	1769.47	1136.24	947.31	866.97	827.84	807.53
85000	1880.06	1207.26	1006.52	921.16	879.58	858.00
90000	1990.65	1278.27	1065.72	975.34	931.32	908.47
95000	2101.25	1349.28	1124.93	1029.53	983.06	958.94
100000	2211.84	1420.30	1184.14	1083.71	1034.80	1009.41

11.00%

Amount	5 Years	10 Years	15 Years	20 Years	25 Years	30 Years
50	1.09	.69	.57	.52	.50	.48
100	2.18	1.38	1.14	1.04	.99	.96
500	10.88	6.89	5.69	5.17	4.91	4.77
1000	21.75	13.78	11.37	10.33	9.81	9.53
2000	43.49	27.56	22.74	20.65	19.61	19.05
5000	108.72	68.88	56.83	51.61	49.01	47.62
10000	217.43	137.76	113.66	103.22	98.02	95.24
15000	326.14	206.63	170.49	154.83	147.02	142.85
20000	434.85	275.51	227.32	206.44	196.03	190.47
25000	543.57	344.38	284.15	258.05	245.03	238.09
30000	652.28	413.26	340.98	309.66	294.04	285.70
35000	760.99	482.13	397.81	361.27	343.04	333.32
40000	869.70	551.01	454.64	412.88	392.05	380.93
45000	978.41	619.88	511.47	464.49	441.06	428.55
50000	1087.13	688.76	568.30	516.10	490.06	476.17
55000	1195.84	757.63	625.13	567.71	539.07	523.78
60000	1304.55	826.51	681.96	619.32	588.07	571.40
65000	1413.26	895.38	738.79	670.93	637.08	619.02
70000	1521.97	964.26	795.62	722.54	686.08	666.63
75000	1630.69	1033.13	852.45	774.15	735.09	714.25
80000	1739.40	1102.01	909.28	825.76	784.10	761.86
85000	1848.11	1170.88	966.11	877.37	833.10	809.48
90000	1956.82	1239.76	1022.94	928.97	882.11	857.10
95000	2065.54	1308.63	1079.77	980.58	931.11	904.71
100000	2174.25	1377.51	1136.60	1032.19	980.12	952.33

11.25%

Amount	5 Years	10 Years	15 Years	20 Years	25 Years	30 Years
50	1.10	.70	.58	.53	.50	.49
100	2.19	1.40	1.16	1.05	1.00	.98
500	10.94	6.96	5.77	5.25	5.00	4.86
1000	21.87	13.92	11.53	10.50	9.99	9.72
2000	43.74	27.84	23.05	20.99	19.97	19.43
5000	109.34	69.59	57.62	52.47	49.92	48.57
10000	218.68	139.17	115.24	104.93	99.83	97.13
15000	328.01	208.76	172.86	157.39	149.74	145.69
20000	437.35	278.34	230.47	209.86	199.65	194.26
25000	546.69	347.93	288.09	262.32	249.56	242.82
30000	656.02	417.51	345.71	314.78	299.48	291.38
35000	765.36	487.10	403.33	367.24	349.39	339.95
40000	874.70	556.68	460.94	419.71	399.30	388.51
45000	984.03	626.27	518.56	472.17	449.21	437.07
50000	1093.37	695.85	576.18	524.63	499.12	485.64
55000	1202.71	765.43	633.79	577.10	549.04	534.20
60000	1312.04	835.02	691.41	629.56	598.95	582.76
65000	1421.38	904.60	749.03	682.02	648.86	631.32
70000	1530.72	974.19	806.65	734.48	698.77	679.89
75000	1640.05	1043.77	864.26	786.95	748.68	728.45
80000	1749.39	1113.36	921.88	839.41	798.60	777.01
85000	1858.73	1182.94	979.50	891.87	848.51	825.58
90000	1968.06	1252.53	1037.12	944.34	898.42	874.14
95000	2077.40	1322.11	1094.73	996.80	948.33	922.70
100000	2186.74	1391.69	1152.35	1049.26	998.24	971.27

APPENDIX B: Amortization Tables: Monthly Payment Necessary To Amortize A Loan

12.00%

Amount	5 Years	10 Years	15 Years	20 Years	25 Years	30 Years
50	1.12	.72	.61	.56	.53	.52
100	2.23	1.44	1.21	1.11	1.06	1.03
500	11.13	7.18	6.01	5.51	5.27	5.15
1000	22.25	14.35	12.01	11.02	10.54	10.29
2000	44.49	28.70	24.01	22.03	21.07	20.58
5000	111.23	71.74	60.01	55.06	52.67	51.44
10000	222.45	143.48	120.02	110.11	105.33	102.87
15000	333.67	215.21	180.03	165.17	157.99	154.30
20000	444.89	286.95	240.04	220.22	210.65	205.73
25000	556.12	358.68	300.05	275.28	263.31	257.16
30000	667.34	430.42	360.06	330.33	315.97	308.59
35000	778.56	502.15	420.06	385.39	368.63	360.02
40000	889.78	573.89	480.07	440.44	421.29	411.45
45000	1001.01	645.62	540.08	495.49	473.96	462.88
50000	1112.23	717.36	600.09	550.55	526.62	514.31
55000	1223.45	789.10	660.10	605.60	579.28	565.74
60000	1334.67	860.83	720.11	660.66	631.94	617.17
65000	1445.89	932.57	780.11	715.71	684.60	668.60
70000	1557.12	1004.30	840.12	770.77	737.26	720.03
75000	1668.34	1076.04	900.13	825.82	789.92	771.46
80000	1779.56	1147.77	960.14	880.87	842.58	822.90
85000	1890.78	1219.51	1020.15	935.93	895.25	874.33
90000	2002.01	1291.24	1080.16	990.98	947.91	925.76
95000	2113.23	1362.98	1140.16	1046.04	1000.57	977.19
100000	2224.45	1434.71	1200.17	1101.09	1053.23	1028.62

12.25%

Amount	5 Years	10 Years	15 Years	20 Years	25 Years	30 Years
50	1.12	.73	.61	.56	.54	.53
100	2.24	1.45	1.22	1.12	1.08	1.05
500	11.19	7.25	6.09	5.60	5.36	5.24
1000	22.38	14.50	12.17	11.19	10.72	10.48
2000	44.75	28.99	24.33	22.38	21.44	20.96
5000	111.86	72.46	60.82	55.93	53.59	52.40
10000	223.71	144.92	121.63	111.86	107.18	104.79
15000	335.57	217.38	182.45	167.79	160.77	157.19
20000	447.42	289.84	243.26	223.72	214.35	209.58
25000	559.28	362.30	304.08	279.65	267.94	261.98
30000	671.13	434.76	364.89	335.57	321.53	314.37
35000	782.99	507.22	425.71	391.50	375.12	366.77
40000	894.84	579.68	486.52	447.43	428.70	419.16
45000	1006.70	652.14	547.34	503.36	482.29	471.56
50000	1118.55	724.60	608.15	559.29	535.88	523.95
55000	1230.41	797.06	668.97	615.22	589.46	576.35
60000	1342.26	869.52	729.78	671.14	643.05	628.74
65000	1454.12	941.98	790.60	727.07	696.64	681.14
70000	1565.97	1014.44	851.41	783.00	750.23	733.53
75000	1677.83	1086.90	912.23	838.93	803.81	785.93
80000	1789.68	1159.36	973.04	894.86	857.40	838.32
85000	1901.54	1231.82	1033.86	950.78	910.99	890.72
90000	2013.39	1304.28	1094.67	1006.71	964.57	943.11
95000	2125.25	1376.74	1155.49	1062.64	1018.16	995.51
100000	2237.10	1449.20	1216.30	1118.57	1071.75	1047.90

12.50%

Amount	5 Years	10 Years	15 Years	20 Years	25 Years	30 Years
50	1.13	.74	.62	.57	.55	.54
100	2.25	1.47	1.24	1.14	1.10	1.07
500	11.25	7.32	6.17	5.69	5.46	5.34
1000	22.50	14.64	12.33	11.37	10.91	10.68
2000	45.00	29.28	24.66	22.73	21.81	21.35
5000	112.49	73.19	61.63	56.81	54.52	53.37
10000	224.98	146.38	123.26	113.62	109.04	106.73
15000	337.47	219.57	184.88	170.43	163.56	160.09
20000	449.96	292.76	246.51	227.23	218.08	213.46
25000	562.45	365.95	308.14	284.04	272.59	266.82
30000	674.94	439.13	369.76	340.85	327.11	320.18
35000	787.43	512.32	431.39	397.65	381.63	373.55
40000	899.92	585.51	493.01	454.46	436.15	426.91
45000	1012.41	658.70	554.64	511.27	490.66	480.27
50000	1124.90	731.89	616.27	568.08	545.18	533.63
55000	1237.39	805.07	677.89	624.88	599.70	587.00
60000	1349.88	878.26	739.52	681.69	654.22	640.36
65000	1462.37	951.45	801.14	738.50	708.74	693.72
70000	1574.86	1024.64	862.77	795.30	763.25	747.09
75000	1687.35	1097.83	924.40	852.11	817.77	800.45
80000	1799.84	1171.01	986.02	908.92	872.29	853.81
85000	1912.33	1244.20	1047.65	965.72	926.81	907.17
90000	2024.82	1317.39	1109.27	1022.53	981.32	960.54
95000	2137.31	1390.58	1170.90	1079.34	1035.84	1013.90
100000	2249.80	1463.77	1232.53	1136.15	1090.36	1067.26

12.75%

Amount	5 Years	10 Years	15 Years	20 Years	25 Years	30 Years
50	1.14	.74	.63	.58	.56	.55
100	2.27	1.48	1.25	1.16	1.11	1.09
500	11.32	7.40	6.25	5.77	5.55	5.44
1000	22.63	14.79	12.49	11.54	11.10	10.87
2000	45.26	29.57	24.98	23.08	22.19	21.74
5000	113.13	73.92	62.45	57.70	55.46	54.34
10000	226.26	147.84	124.89	115.39	110.91	108.67
15000	339.38	221.76	187.33	173.08	166.36	163.01
20000	452.51	295.68	249.77	230.77	221.82	217.34
25000	565.64	369.60	312.21	288.46	277.27	271.68
30000	678.76	443.52	374.66	346.15	332.72	326.01
35000	791.89	517.44	437.10	403.84	388.17	380.35
40000	905.02	591.36	499.54	461.53	443.63	434.68
45000	1018.14	665.28	561.98	519.22	499.08	489.02
50000	1131.27	739.20	624.42	576.91	554.53	543.35
55000	1244.40	813.12	686.87	634.60	609.98	597.69
60000	1357.52	887.04	749.31	692.29	665.44	652.02
65000	1470.65	960.96	811.75	749.98	720.89	706.36
70000	1583.78	1034.88	874.19	807.67	776.34	760.69
75000	1696.90	1108.80	936.63	865.36	831.79	815.02
80000	1810.03	1182.72	999.07	923.05	887.25	869.36
85000	1923.16	1256.64	1061.52	980.74	942.70	923.69
90000	2036.28	1330.56	1123.96	1038.44	998.15	978.03
95000	2149.41	1404.48	1186.40	1096.13	1053.60	1032.36
100000	2262.54	1478.40	1248.84	1153.82	1109.06	1086.70

13.00%

Amount	5 Years	10 Years	15 Years	20 Years	25 Years	30 Years
50	1.14	.75	.64	.59	.57	.56
100	2.28	1.50	1.27	1.18	1.13	1.11
500	11.38	7.47	6.33	5.86	5.64	5.54
1000	22.76	14.94	12.66	11.72	11.28	11.07
2000	45.51	29.87	25.31	23.44	22.56	22.13
5000	113.77	74.66	63.27	58.58	56.40	55.31
10000	227.54	149.32	126.53	117.16	112.79	110.62
15000	341.30	223.97	189.79	175.74	169.18	165.93
20000	455.07	298.63	253.05	234.32	225.57	221.24
25000	568.83	373.28	316.32	292.90	281.96	276.55
30000	682.60	447.94	379.58	351.48	338.36	331.86
35000	796.36	522.59	442.84	410.06	394.75	387.17
40000	910.13	597.25	506.10	468.64	451.14	442.48
45000	1023.89	671.90	569.36	527.21	507.53	497.79
50000	1137.66	746.56	632.63	585.79	563.92	553.10
55000	1251.42	821.21	695.89	644.37	620.31	608.41
60000	1365.19	895.87	759.15	702.95	676.71	663.72
65000	1478.95	970.52	822.41	761.53	733.10	719.03
70000	1592.72	1045.18	885.67	820.11	789.49	774.34
75000	1706.49	1119.84	948.94	878.69	845.88	829.65
80000	1820.25	1194.49	1012.20	937.27	902.27	884.96
85000	1934.02	1269.15	1075.46	995.84	958.67	940.27
90000	2047.78	1343.80	1138.72	1054.42	1015.06	995.58
95000	2161.55	1418.46	1201.99	1113.00	1071.45	1050.89
100000	2275.31	1493.11	1265.25	1171.58	1127.84	1106.20

13.25%

Amount	5 Years	10 Years	15 Years	20 Years	25 Years	30 Years
50	1.15	.76	.65	.60	.58	.57
100	2.29	1.51	1.29	1.19	1.15	1.13
500	11.45	7.54	6.41	5.95	5.74	5.63
1000	22.89	15.08	12.82	11.90	11.47	11.26
2000	45.77	30.16	25.64	23.79	22.94	22.52
5000	114.41	75.40	64.09	59.48	57.34	56.29
10000	228.82	150.79	128.18	118.95	114.68	112.58
15000	343.22	226.19	192.27	178.42	172.01	168.87
20000	457.63	301.58	256.35	237.89	229.35	225.16
25000	572.04	376.98	320.44	297.36	286.68	281.45
30000	686.44	452.37	384.53	356.83	344.02	337.74
35000	800.85	527.77	448.61	416.31	401.35	394.03
40000	915.26	603.16	512.70	475.78	458.69	450.31
45000	1029.66	678.56	576.79	535.25	516.02	506.60
50000	1144.07	753.95	640.87	594.72	573.36	562.89
55000	1258.47	829.34	704.96	654.19	630.69	619.18
60000	1372.88	904.74	769.05	713.66	688.03	675.47
65000	1487.29	980.13	833.13	773.13	745.36	731.76
70000	1601.69	1055.53	897.22	832.61	802.70	788.05
75000	1716.10	1130.92	961.31	892.08	860.03	844.34
80000	1830.51	1206.32	1025.39	951.55	917.37	900.62
85000	1944.91	1281.71	1089.48	1011.02	974.70	956.91
90000	2059.32	1357.11	1153.57	1070.49	1032.04	1013.20
95000	2173.72	1432.50	1217.65	1129.96	1089.37	1069.49
100000	2288.12	1507.89	1281.74	1189.44	1146.71	1125.78

13.50%

Amount	5 Years	10 Years	15 Years	20 Years	25 Years	30 Years
50	1.16	.77	.65	.61	.59	.58
100	2.31	1.53	1.30	1.21	1.17	1.15
500	11.51	7.62	6.50	6.04	5.83	5.73
1000	23.01	15.23	12.99	12.08	11.66	11.46
2000	46.02	30.46	25.97	24.15	23.32	22.91
5000	115.05	76.14	64.92	60.37	58.29	57.28
10000	230.10	152.28	129.84	120.74	116.57	114.55
15000	345.15	228.42	194.75	181.11	174.85	171.82
20000	460.20	304.55	259.67	241.48	233.13	229.09
25000	575.25	380.69	324.58	301.85	291.42	286.36
30000	690.30	456.83	389.50	362.22	349.70	343.63
35000	805.35	532.97	454.42	422.59	407.98	400.90
40000	920.40	609.10	519.33	482.95	466.26	458.17
45000	1035.45	685.24	584.25	543.32	524.55	515.44
50000	1150.50	761.38	649.16	603.69	582.83	572.71
55000	1265.55	837.51	714.08	664.06	641.11	629.98
60000	1380.60	913.65	779.00	724.43	699.39	687.25
65000	1495.65	989.79	843.91	784.80	757.67	744.52
70000	1610.69	1065.93	908.83	845.17	815.96	801.79
75000	1725.74	1142.06	973.74	905.54	874.24	859.06
80000	1840.79	1218.20	1038.66	965.90	932.52	916.33
85000	1955.84	1294.34	1103.58	1026.27	990.80	973.61
90000	2070.89	1370.47	1168.49	1086.64	1049.09	1030.88
95000	2185.94	1446.61	1233.41	1147.01	1107.37	1088.15
100000	2300.99	1522.75	1298.32	1207.38	1165.65	1145.42

13.75%

Amount	5 Years	10 Years	15 Years	20 Years	25 Years	30 Years
50	1.16	.77	.66	.62	.60	.59
100	2.32	1.54	1.32	1.23	1.19	1.17
500	11.57	7.69	6.58	6.13	5.93	5.83
1000	23.14	15.38	13.15	12.26	11.85	11.66
2000	46.28	30.76	26.30	24.51	23.70	23.31
5000	115.70	76.89	65.75	61.28	59.24	58.26
10000	231.39	153.77	131.49	122.55	118.47	116.52
15000	347.09	230.66	197.25	183.82	177.70	174.77
20000	462.78	307.54	263.00	245.09	236.94	233.03
25000	578.48	384.42	328.75	306.36	296.17	291.28
30000	694.17	461.31	394.50	367.63	355.40	349.54
35000	809.86	538.19	460.25	428.90	414.64	407.79
40000	925.56	615.07	526.00	490.17	473.87	466.05
45000	1041.25	691.96	591.75	551.44	533.10	524.31
50000	1156.95	768.84	657.50	612.71	592.34	582.56
55000	1272.64	845.72	723.25	673.98	651.57	640.82
60000	1388.34	922.61	789.00	735.25	710.80	699.07
65000	1504.03	999.49	854.75	796.52	770.04	757.33
70000	1619.72	1076.37	920.50	857.79	829.27	815.58
75000	1735.42	1153.26	986.25	919.06	888.50	873.84
80000	1851.11	1230.14	1051.99	980.33	947.74	932.10
85000	1966.81	1307.02	1117.74	1041.60	1006.97	990.35
90000	2082.50	1383.91	1183.49	1102.87	1066.20	1048.61
95000	2198.20	1460.79	1249.24	1164.14	1125.44	1106.86
100000	2313.89	1537.67	1314.99	1225.41	1184.67	1165.12

APPENDIX B: Amortization Tables: Monthly Payment Necessary To Amortize A Loan

14.50%

Amount	5 Years	10 Years	15 Years	20 Years	25 Years	30 Years
50	1.18	.80	.69	.64	.63	.62
100	2.36	1.59	1.37	1.28	1.25	1.23
500	11.77	7.92	6.83	6.40	6.22	6.13
1000	23.53	15.83	13.66	12.80	12.43	12.25
2000	47.06	31.66	27.32	25.60	24.85	24.50
5000	117.65	79.15	68.28	64.00	62.11	61.23
10000	235.29	158.29	136.56	128.00	124.22	122.46
15000	352.93	237.44	204.83	192.00	186.33	183.69
20000	470.57	316.58	273.11	256.00	248.44	244.92
25000	588.21	395.72	341.38	320.00	310.55	306.14
30000	705.85	474.87	409.66	384.00	372.65	367.37
35000	823.49	554.01	477.93	448.00	434.76	428.60
40000	941.14	633.15	546.21	512.00	496.87	489.83
45000	1058.78	712.30	614.48	576.00	558.98	551.06
50000	1176.42	791.44	682.76	640.00	621.09	612.28
55000	1294.06	870.58	751.03	704.00	683.19	673.51
60000	1411.70	949.73	819.31	768.00	745.30	734.74
65000	1529.34	1028.87	887.58	832.00	807.41	795.97
70000	1646.98	1108.01	955.86	896.00	869.52	857.19
75000	1764.63	1187.16	1024.13	960.00	931.63	918.42
80000	1882.27	1266.30	1092.41	1024.00	993.74	979.65
85000	1999.91	1345.44	1160.68	1088.00	1055.84	1040.88
90000	2117.55	1424.59	1228.96	1152.00	1117.95	1102.11
95000	2235.19	1503.73	1297.23	1216.00	1180.06	1163.33
100000	2352.83	1582.87	1365.51	1280.00	1242.17	1224.56

14.75%

Amount	5 Years	10 Years	15 Years	20 Years	25 Years	30 Years
50	1.19	.80	.70	.65	.64	.63
100	2.37	1.60	1.39	1.30	1.27	1.25
500	11.83	8.00	6.92	6.50	6.31	6.23
1000	23.66	15.99	13.83	12.99	12.62	12.45
2000	47.32	31.97	27.66	25.97	25.23	24.89
5000	118.30	79.91	69.13	64.92	63.08	62.23
10000	236.59	159.81	138.26	129.84	126.15	124.45
15000	354.89	239.72	207.38	194.76	189.22	186.68
20000	473.18	319.62	276.51	259.68	252.30	248.90
25000	591.48	399.52	345.63	324.59	315.37	311.12
30000	709.77	479.43	414.76	389.51	378.44	373.35
35000	828.07	559.33	483.88	454.43	441.52	435.57
40000	946.36	639.23	553.01	519.35	504.59	497.80
45000	1064.66	719.14	622.13	584.26	567.66	560.02
50000	1182.95	799.04	691.26	649.18	630.74	622.24
55000	1301.24	878.95	760.38	714.10	693.81	684.47
60000	1419.54	958.85	829.51	779.02	756.88	746.69
65000	1537.83	1038.75	898.63	843.94	819.96	808.91
70000	1656.13	1118.66	967.76	908.85	883.03	871.14
75000	1774.42	1198.56	1036.88	973.77	946.10	933.36
80000	1892.72	1278.46	1106.01	1038.69	1009.18	995.59
85000	2011.01	1358.37	1175.13	1103.61	1072.25	1057.81
90000	2129.31	1438.27	1244.26	1168.52	1135.32	1120.03
95000	2247.60	1518.18	1313.38	1233.44	1198.40	1182.26
100000	2365.90	1598.08	1382.51	1298.36	1261.47	1244.48

14.00%

Amount	5 Years	10 Years	15 Years	20 Years	25 Years	30 Years
50	1.17	.78	.67	.63	.61	.60
100	2.33	1.56	1.34	1.25	1.21	1.19
500	11.64	7.77	6.66	6.22	6.02	5.93
1000	23.27	15.53	13.32	12.44	12.04	11.85
2000	46.54	31.06	26.64	24.88	24.08	23.70
5000	116.35	77.64	66.59	62.18	60.19	59.25
10000	232.69	155.27	133.18	124.36	120.38	118.49
15000	349.03	232.90	199.77	186.53	180.57	177.74
20000	465.37	310.54	266.35	248.71	240.76	236.98
25000	581.71	388.17	332.94	310.89	300.95	296.22
30000	698.05	465.80	399.53	373.06	361.13	355.47
35000	814.39	543.44	466.11	435.24	421.32	414.71
40000	930.74	621.07	532.70	497.41	481.51	473.95
45000	1047.08	698.70	599.29	559.59	541.70	533.20
50000	1163.42	776.34	665.88	621.77	601.89	592.44
55000	1279.76	853.97	732.46	683.94	662.07	651.68
60000	1396.10	931.60	799.05	746.12	722.26	710.17
65000	1512.44	1009.24	865.64	808.29	782.45	770.17
70000	1628.78	1086.87	932.22	870.47	842.64	829.42
75000	1745.12	1164.50	998.81	932.65	902.83	888.66
80000	1861.47	1242.14	1065.40	994.82	963.01	947.90
85000	1977.81	1319.77	1131.99	1057.00	1023.20	1007.15
90000	2094.15	1397.40	1198.57	1119.17	1083.39	1066.39
95000	2210.49	1475.04	1265.16	1181.35	1143.58	1125.63
100000	2326.83	1552.67	1331.75	1243.53	1203.77	1184.88

14.25%

Amount	5 Years	10 Years	15 Years	20 Years	25 Years	30 Years
50	1.17	.79	.68	.64	.62	.61
100	2.34	1.57	1.35	1.27	1.23	1.21
500	11.70	7.84	6.75	6.31	6.12	6.03
1000	23.40	15.68	13.49	12.62	12.23	12.05
2000	46.80	31.36	26.98	25.24	24.46	24.10
5000	117.00	78.39	67.43	63.09	61.15	60.24
10000	233.99	156.78	134.86	126.18	122.30	120.47
15000	350.98	235.16	202.29	189.26	183.44	180.71
20000	467.97	313.55	269.72	252.35	244.59	240.94
25000	584.96	391.94	337.15	315.43	305.74	301.18
30000	701.95	470.32	404.58	378.52	366.88	361.41
35000	818.94	548.71	472.01	441.61	428.03	421.65
40000	935.93	627.10	539.44	504.69	489.18	481.88
45000	1052.92	705.48	606.87	567.78	550.32	542.11
50000	1169.91	783.87	674.29	630.86	611.47	602.35
55000	1286.90	862.26	741.72	693.95	672.62	662.58
60000	1403.89	940.64	809.15	757.04	733.76	722.82
65000	1520.88	1019.03	876.58	820.12	794.91	783.05
70000	1637.88	1097.42	944.01	883.21	856.05	843.29
75000	1754.86	1175.80	1011.44	946.29	917.20	903.52
80000	1871.85	1254.19	1078.87	1009.38	978.35	963.75
85000	1988.84	1332.58	1146.30	1072.47	1039.49	1023.99
90000	2105.83	1410.96	1213.73	1135.55	1100.64	1084.22
95000	2222.82	1489.35	1281.16	1198.64	1161.79	1144.46
100000	2339.81	1567.74	1348.58	1261.72	1222.93	1204.69

15.50%

Amount	5 Years	10 Years	15 Years	20 Years	25 Years	30 Years
50	1.21	.83	.72	.68	.66	.66
100	2.41	1.65	1.44	1.36	1.32	1.31
500	12.03	8.23	7.17	6.77	6.60	6.53
1000	24.06	16.45	14.34	13.54	13.20	13.05
2000	48.11	32.89	28.68	27.08	26.40	26.10
5000	120.27	82.21	71.70	67.70	65.99	65.23
10000	240.54	164.42	143.40	135.39	131.98	130.46
15000	360.80	246.62	215.10	203.09	197.97	195.68
20000	481.07	328.83	286.80	270.78	263.95	260.91
25000	601.33	411.03	358.50	338.48	329.94	326.13
30000	721.60	493.24	430.20	406.17	395.93	391.36
35000	841.87	575.44	501.90	473.86	461.92	456.59
40000	962.13	657.65	573.60	541.56	527.90	521.81
45000	1082.40	739.85	645.30	609.25	593.89	587.04
50000	1202.66	822.06	717.00	676.95	659.88	652.26
55000	1322.93	904.26	788.70	744.64	725.86	717.49
60000	1443.20	986.47	860.40	812.33	791.85	782.72
65000	1563.46	1068.67	932.10	880.03	857.84	847.94
70000	1683.73	1150.88	1003.80	947.72	923.83	913.17
75000	1803.99	1233.08	1075.50	1015.42	989.81	978.39
80000	1924.26	1315.29	1147.20	1083.11	1055.80	1043.62
85000	2044.53	1397.49	1218.90	1150.80	1121.79	1108.84
90000	2164.79	1479.70	1290.60	1218.50	1187.78	1174.07
95000	2285.06	1561.91	1362.30	1286.19	1253.76	1239.30
100000	2405.32	1644.11	1434.00	1353.89	1319.75	1304.52

15.00%

Amount	5 Years	10 Years	15 Years	20 Years	25 Years	30 Years
50	1.19	.81	.70	.66	.65	.64
100	2.38	1.62	1.40	1.32	1.29	1.27
500	11.90	8.07	7.00	6.59	6.41	6.33
1000	23.79	16.14	14.00	13.17	12.81	12.65
2000	47.58	32.27	28.00	26.34	25.62	25.29
5000	118.95	80.67	69.98	65.84	64.05	63.23
10000	237.90	161.34	139.96	131.68	128.09	126.45
15000	356.85	242.01	209.94	197.52	192.13	189.67
20000	475.80	322.67	279.92	263.36	256.17	252.89
25000	594.75	403.34	349.90	329.20	320.21	316.12
30000	713.70	484.01	419.88	395.04	384.25	379.34
35000	832.65	564.68	489.86	460.88	448.30	442.56
40000	951.60	645.34	559.84	526.72	512.34	505.78
45000	1070.55	726.01	629.82	592.56	576.38	569.00
50000	1189.50	806.68	699.80	658.40	640.42	632.23
55000	1308.45	887.35	769.78	724.24	704.46	695.45
60000	1427.40	968.01	839.76	790.08	768.50	758.67
65000	1546.35	1048.68	909.74	855.92	832.54	821.89
70000	1665.30	1129.35	979.72	921.76	896.59	885.12
75000	1784.25	1210.02	1049.70	987.60	960.63	948.34
80000	1903.20	1290.68	1119.67	1053.44	1024.67	1011.56
85000	2022.15	1371.35	1189.65	1119.28	1088.71	1074.78
90000	2141.10	1452.02	1259.63	1185.12	1152.75	1138.00
95000	2260.05	1532.69	1329.61	1250.96	1216.79	1201.23
100000	2379.00	1613.35	1399.59	1316.79	1280.84	1264.45

15.25%

Amount	5 Years	10 Years	15 Years	20 Years	25 Years	30 Years
50	1.20	.82	.71	.67	.66	.65
100	2.40	1.63	1.42	1.34	1.31	1.29
500	11.97	8.15	7.09	6.68	6.51	6.43
1000	23.93	16.29	14.17	13.36	13.01	12.85
2000	47.85	32.58	28.34	26.71	26.01	25.69
5000	119.61	81.44	70.84	66.77	65.02	64.23
10000	239.22	162.87	141.68	133.53	130.03	128.45
15000	358.83	244.31	212.52	200.30	195.04	192.67
20000	478.43	325.74	283.35	267.06	260.06	256.90
25000	598.04	407.18	354.19	333.83	325.07	321.12
30000	717.65	488.61	425.03	400.59	390.08	385.34
35000	837.25	570.05	495.87	467.36	455.10	449.57
40000	956.86	651.48	566.70	534.12	520.11	513.79
45000	1076.47	732.92	637.54	600.89	585.12	578.01
50000	1196.07	814.35	708.38	667.65	650.13	642.23
55000	1315.68	895.79	779.22	734.42	715.15	706.46
60000	1435.29	977.22	850.05	801.18	780.16	770.68
65000	1554.89	1058.66	920.89	867.95	845.17	834.90
70000	1674.50	1140.09	991.73	934.71	910.19	899.13
75000	1794.11	1221.53	1062.57	1001.48	975.20	963.35
80000	1913.71	1302.96	1133.40	1068.24	1040.21	1027.57
85000	2033.32	1384.39	1204.24	1135.01	1105.22	1091.79
90000	2152.93	1465.83	1275.08	1201.77	1170.24	1156.02
95000	2272.53	1547.26	1345.92	1268.54	1235.25	1220.24
100000	2392.14	1628.70	1416.75	1335.30	1300.26	1284.46

APPENDIX **C**

APPENDIX C: TABLES OF OUTSTANDING BALANCES

How To Read The Tables In Appendix C

Appendix C tables show the amount of outstanding debt (unpaid balance) still remaining on your mortgage at particular points in time during your loan term—after 5, 10, 15, 20, 25, and 30 years of making payments.

To figure out the outstanding debt (balance) on your mortgage at a given point in time (at the 5, 10, 15, 20, 25, and 30-year points), here's what you do: (1) refer to the table having the applicable interest rate for your mortgage (if your rate happens to fall in-between the quarter-percentage rate tables listed, estimate your remaining balance figure as an average of the rates above and below your rate, as explained in Chapter 9); (2) select from the first column of the table (the "age of loan"), the line corresponding to the number of years that you've had the house or held the mortgage; (3) look at the number of years listed on top of each column. One of these numbers, the particular one that applies to you, represents the original term for your mortgage loan—the number of years for which you originally took out the loan; now, the percentage shown under the "years" column on the line corresponding to the age of you loan, is the proportion of the loan still remaining on your loan. For example, let's say the applicable age of your loan (the number of years you've held the mortgage) is 10 years; your loan was for $100,000, 30-year term at 10 percent interest. Reading from the "age of loan" column in the 10 percent table, the percentage shown for age 10 is 90.94. Therefore, on a $100,000 original mortgage, what you still owe today, after 10 years of paying on the loan, is about $90,940, as follows:

$$\$100,000 \times 90.94 = \$90,940$$

8.00%

Age of Loan	5 years	10 years	15 years	20 years	25 years	30 years
1	83.06	93.19	96.40	97.89	98.69	99.16
2	64.71	85.82	92.51	95.60	97.27	98.26
3	44.83	77.84	88.29	93.12	95.71	97.27
4	23.31	69.20	83.72	90.43	94.07	96.22
5	0	59.84	78.77	87.53	92.27	95.07
6		49.70	73.41	84.38	90.32	93.83
7		38.72	67.60	80.97	88.21	92.48
8		26.83	61.31	77.27	85.92	91.02
9		13.95	54.51	73.27	83.45	89.44
10		0	47.13	68.94	80.76	87.72
11			39.15	64.25	77.86	85.87
12			30.50	59.17	74.71	83.86
13			21.13	53.67	71.30	81.69
14			10.99	47.71	67.61	79.33
15			0	41.25	63.61	76.78
16				34.26	59.29	74.02
17				26.69	54.60	71.03
18				18.49	49.52	67.79
19				9.62	44.02	64.28
20				0	38.06	60.48
21					31.62	56.36
22					24.63	51.91
23					17.07	47.08
24					8.87	41.85
25					0	36.19
26						30.06
27						23.42
28						16.22
29						8.44
30						0

8.25%

Age of Loan	5 years	10 years	15 years	20 years	25 years	30 years
1	83.15	93.28	96.48	97.95	98.74	99.21
2	64.85	85.99	92.65	95.72	97.38	98.34
3	44.98	78.07	88.50	93.30	95.89	97.41
4	23.42	69.47	83.99	90.68	94.28	96.39
5	0	60.13	79.10	87.83	92.53	95.28
6		50.00	73.78	84.73	90.64	94.09
7		39.00	68.01	81.38	88.58	92.78
8		27.05	61.75	77.73	86.34	91.37
9		14.08	54.97	73.91	83.91	89.84
10		0	47.56	69.47	81.27	88.17
11			39.55	64.80	78.41	86.36
12			30.85	59.74	75.30	84.40
13			21.40	54.23	71.93	82.27
14			11.14	48.26	68.26	79.95
15			0.	41.78	64.28	77.44
16				34.74	59.96	74.71
17				27.09	55.28	71.75
18				18.79	50.18	68.53
19				9.78	44.66	65.04
20				0	38.66	61.25
21					32.14	57.14
22					25.07	52.67
23					17.39	47.82
24					9.05	42.55
25					0	36.83
26						30.63
27						23.89
28						16.57
29						8.62
30						0

8.50%

Age of Loan	5 years	10 years	15 years	20 years	25 years	30 years
1	83.24	93.37	96.55	98.01	98.70	99.24
2	64.99	86.15	92.80	95.84	97.47	98.42
3	45.14	78.29	88.71	93.49	96.04	97.53
4	23.52	69.74	84.26	90.92	94.48	96.55
5	0.	60.43	79.42	88.13	92.79	95.49
6		50.30	74.16	85.09	90.94	94.34
7		39.28	68.42	81.78	88.93	93.08
8		27.28	62.18	78.18	86.14	91.71
9		14.22	55.39	74.26	84.36	90.22
10		0	48.00	69.99	81.77	88.60
11			39.95	65.35	78.95	86.84
12			31.19	60.30	75.88	84.92
13			21.66	54.80	72.54	82.83
14			11.29	48.81	68.90	80.56
15			0	42.30	64.95	78.08
16				35.21	60.64	75.39
17				27.49	55.95	72.46
18				19.09	50.85	69.27
19				9.95	45.29	65.80
20				0	39.25	62.02
21					32.67	57.90
22					25.51	53.43
23					17.71	48.55
24					9.23	43.25
25					0	37.48
26						31.20
27						24.36
28						16.92
29						8.82
30						0

8.75%

Age of Loan	5 years	10 years	15 years	20 years	25 years	30 years
1	83.33	93.45	96.62	98.07	98.84	99.28
2	65.14	86.31	92.94	95.96	97.57	98.70
3	45.29	78.51	88.92	93.66	96.19	97.41
4	23.63	70.01	84.54	91.16	94.68	96.71
5	0	60.73	79.75	88.42	93.03	95.69
6		50.60	74.53	85.43	91.24	94.58
7		39.56	68.83	82.18	89.28	93.34
8		27.50	62.61	78.62	87.14	92.04
9		14.35	55.83	74.74	84.81	90.60
10		0	48.43	70.51	82.26	89.02
11			40.35	65.90	79.48	87.30
12			31.54	60.86	76.45	85.43
13			21.93	55.36	73.14	83.38
14			11.44	49.36	69.54	81.15
15			0	42.82	65.60	78.77
16				35.68	61.30	76.06
17				27.89	56.62	73.16
18				19.39	51.50	69.99
19				10.12	45.93	66.54
20				0	39.84	62.77
21					33.20	58.66
22					25.95	54.18
23					18.04	49.28
24					9.41	43.95
25					0	38.12
26						31.76
27						24.83
28						17.26
29						9.01
30						0

APPENDIX C: Loan Progress Chart: Table Of Remaining Balances

9.00%

Age of Loan	5 years	10 years	15 years	20 years	25 years	30 years
1	83.42	93.54	96.69	98.13	98.88	99.32
2	65.28	86.47	93.08	96.08	97.66	98.57
3	45.44	78.73	89.12	93.84	96.33	97.75
4	23.74	70.28	84.80	91.39	94.87	96.86
5	0	61.02	80.07	88.71	93.27	95.88
6		50.90	74.89	85.77	91.53	94.81
7		39.84	69.23	82.57	89.62	93.64
8		27.73	63.04	79.06	87.53	92.36
9		14.49	56.27	75.22	85.24	90.96
10		0	48.86	71.03	82.74	89.43
11			40.76	66.44	80.00	87.75
12			31.90	61.41	77.01	85.92
13			22.20	55.92	73.74	83.92
14			11.60	49.91	70.16	81.73
15			0	43.34	66.25	79.33
16				36.16	61.97	76.71
17				28.29	57.28	73.84
18				19.69	52.16	70.70
19				10.29	46.56	67.27
20				0	40.43	63.52
21					33.72	59.41
22					26.39	54.92
23					18.37	50.01
24					9.60	44.64
25					0	38.76
26						32.33
27						25.30
28						17.61
29						9.20
30						0

9.25%

Age of Loan	5 years	10 years	15 years	20 years	25 years	30 years
1	83.51	93.62	96.76	98.18	98.93	99.35
2	65.42	86.62	93.22	96.19	97.75	98.64
3	45.59	78.95	89.33	94.01	96.47	97.86
4	23.84	70.54	85.06	91.61	95.05	97.00
5	0	61.32	80.39	88.99	93.51	96.06
6		51.21	75.26	86.11	91.81	95.04
7		40.12	69.63	82.95	89.94	93.91
8		27.96	63.47	79.49	87.90	92.67
9		14.62	56.71	75.70	85.66	91.31
10		0	49.29	71.53	83.21	89.82
11			41.16	66.97	80.52	88.19
12			32.25	61.97	77.57	86.40
13			22.47	56.48	74.33	84.44
14			11.75	50.46	70.78	82.29
15			0	43.86	66.89	79.93
16				36.63	62.62	77.35
17				28.70	57.94	74.51
18				20.00	52.81	71.40
19				10.46	47.18	67.99
20				0	41.01	64.26
21					34.25	60.16
22					26.83	55.66
23					18.70	50.73
24					9.78	45.33
25					0	39.40
26						32.90
27						25.78
28						17.96
29						9.39
30						0

9.50%

Age of Loan	5 years	10 years	15 years	20 years	25 years	30 years
1	83.60	93.70	96.83	98.24	98.97	99.38
2	65.56	86.78	93.35	96.30	97.84	98.71
3	45.74	79.17	89.53	94.18	96.60	97.96
4	23.95	70.81	85.32	91.84	95.23	97.14
5	0	61.61	80.70	89.27	93.73	96.24
6		51.51	75.62	86.44	92.08	95.25
7		40.40	70.03	83.33	90.27	94.16
8		28.18	63.89	79.92	88.27	92.97
9		14.76	57.14	76.16	86.08	91.65
10		0	49.72	72.04	83.67	90.21
11			41.56	67.50	81.02	88.62
12			32.60	62.51	78.11	86.87
13			22.74	57.03	74.91	84.95
14			11.91	51.01	71.39	82.84
15			0	44.38	67.52	80.52
16				37.10	63.27	77.97
17				29.10	58.59	75.17
18				20.30	53.46	72.09
19				10.63	47.81	68.70
20				0	41.60	64.98
21					34.78	60.89
22					27.27	56.39
23					19.03	51.45
24					9.96	46.01
25					0	40.04
26						33.47
27						26.25
28						18.31
29						9.59
30						0

9.75%

Age of Loan	5 years	10 years	15 years	20 years	25 years	30 years
1	83.68	93.78	96.90	98.29	99.01	99.41
2	65.70	86.94	93.49	96.41	97.93	98.77
3	45.89	79.39	89.72	94.34	96.73	98.06
4	24.06	71.07	85.58	92.05	95.41	97.27
5	0	61.91	81.01	89.54	93.95	96.41
6		51.81	75.97	86.76	92.35	95.46
7		40.68	70.43	83.71	90.58	94.41
8		28.41	64.31	80.34	88.63	93.26
9		14.89	57.57	76.62	86.49	91.98
10		0	50.15	72.53	84.12	90.58
11			41.97	68.02	81.51	89.03
12			32.95	63.06	78.64	87.33
13			23.01	57.58	75.48	85.45
14			12.07	51.55	71.99	83.38
15			0	44.90	68.15	81.10
16				37.58	63.91	78.59
17				29.50	59.24	75.82
18				20.61	54.10	72.77
19				10.80	48.43	69.41
20				0	42.19	65.70
21					35.30	61.62
22					27.72	57.12
23					19.36	52.16
24					10.15	46.69
25					0	40.67
26						34.04
27						26.72
28						18.67
29						9.79
30						0

10.50%

Age of Loan	5 years	10 years	15 years	20 years	25 years	30 years
1	83.95	94.03	97.10	98.45	99.13	99.50
2	66.13	87.39	93.88	96.72	98.16	98.94
3	46.35	80.03	90.30	94.81	97.09	98.33
4	24.38	71.85	86.33	92.68	95.90	97.64
5	0	62.78	81.92	90.32	94.57	96.88
6		52.70	77.03	87.70	93.10	96.04
7		41.52	71.59	84.79	91.47	95.10
8		29.10	65.56	81.56	89.66	94.06
9		15.31	58.86	77.97	87.65	92.90
10		0	51.43	73.99	85.42	91.62
11			43.17	69.57	82.94	90.20
12			34.01	64.66	80.19	88.62
13			23.84	59.21	77.13	86.86
14			12.54	53.16	73.74	84.91
15			0	46.45	69.97	82.75
16				38.99	55.79	80.35
17				30.72	61.15	77.68
18				21.53	56.00	74.73
19				11.33	50.28	71.44
20				0	43.93	67.79
21					36.88	63.74
22					29.05	59.24
23					20.36	54.25
24					10.71	48.71
25					0	42.56
26						35.73
27						28.14
28						19.72
29						10.38
30						0

10.75%

Age of Loan	5 years	10 years	15 years	20 years	25 years	30 years
1	84.04	94.10	97.16	98.49	99.16	99.53
2	66.27	87.54	94.00	96.82	98.23	99.00
3	46.50	80.24	90.49	94.95	97.20	98.41
4	24.49	72.11	86.57	92.88	96.05	97.75
5	0	63.07	82.22	90.57	94.77	97.03
6		53.00	77.37	88.00	93.34	96.22
7		41.80	71.98	85.14	91.75	95.31
8		29.33	65.97	81.95	89.98	94.31
9		15.45	59.29	78.41	88.02	93.19
10		0	51.85	74.46	85.83	91.95
11			43.58	70.07	83.39	90.56
12			34.36	65.19	80.68	89.02
13			24.11	59.75	77.66	87.31
14			12.70	53.70	74.30	85.40
15			0	46.96	70.57	83.28
16				39.47	66.41	80.91
17				31.12	61.78	78.28
18				21.84	56.62	75.35
19				11.50	50.89	72.09
20				0	44.50	68.47
21					37.40	64.43
22					29.49	59.94
23					20.69	54.94
24					10.90	49.37
25					0	43.18
26						36.29
27						28.62
28						20.08
29						10.58
30						0

10.00%

Age of Loan	5 years	10 years	15 years	20 years	25 years	30 years
1	83.77	93.87	96.97	98.35	99.05	99.44
2	65.85	87.09	93.62	96.52	98.01	98.83
3	46.04	79.60	89.92	94.50	96.85	98.15
4	24.17	71.33	85.83	92.27	95.57	97.40
5	0	62.20	81.32	89.80	94.16	96.57
6		52.10	76.33	87.08	92.61	95.66
7		40.96	70.82	84.07	90.88	94.65
8		28.64	64.73	80.75	88.98	93.53
9		15.03	58.01	77.08	86.88	92.30
10		0	50.58	73.02	84.56	90.94
11			42.37	68.54	82.00	89.43
12			33.30	63.60	79.17	87.77
13			23.29	58.13	76.04	85.93
14			12.22	52.09	72.58	83.91
15			0	45.42	68.76	81.66
16				38.05	64.54	79.19
17				29.91	59.88	76.45
18				20.91	54.74	73.43
19				10.98	49.05	70.09
20				0	42.77	66.41
21					35.83	62.33
22					28.16	57.83
23					19.69	52.86
24					10.34	47.37
25					0	41.30
26						34.60
27						27.20
28						19.02
29						9.98
30						0

10.25%

Age of Loan	5 years	10 years	15 years	20 years	25 years	30 years
1	83.86	93.95	97.03	98.40	99.09	99.47
2	65.99	87.24	93.75	96.62	98.09	98.89
3	46.20	79.82	90.11	94.65	96.97	98.24
4	24.28	71.59	86.08	92.48	95.74	97.52
5	0	62.49	81.62	90.06	94.37	96.73
6		52.40	76.68	87.39	92.86	95.85
7		41.24	71.21	84.43	91.18	94.88
8		28.87	65.15	81.16	89.33	93.80
9		15.17	58.44	77.53	87.27	92.61
10		0	51.00	73.51	84.99	91.29
11			42.77	69.06	82.47	89.82
12			33.66	64.13	79.68	88.20
13			23.56	58.67	76.59	86.41
14			12.38	52.63	73.16	84.42
15			0	45.94	69.37	82.21
16				38.52	65.17	79.78
17				30.31	60.52	77.08
18				21.22	55.37	74.08
19				11.15	49.67	70.77
20				0	43.35	67.10
21					36.35	63.04
22					28.61	58.54
23					20.03	53.56
24					10.52	48.04
25					0	41.93
26						35.16
27						27.67
28						19.37
29						10.18
30						0

APPENDIX C: Loan Progress Chart: Table Of Remaining Balances

11.00%

Age of Loan	5 years	10 years	15 years	20 years	25 years	30 years
1	84.12	94.18	97.22	98.54	99.20	99.55
2	66.41	87.69	94.13	96.91	98.31	99.05
3	46.65	80.45	90.67	95.10	97.31	98.49
4	24.60	72.37	86.81	93.07	96.20	97.86
5	0	63.36	82.51	90.81	94.95	97.16
6		53.30	77.71	88.29	93.57	96.39
7		42.08	72.36	85.48	92.03	95.52
8		29.56	66.38	82.34	90.30	94.55
9		15.59	59.71	78.84	88.38	93.47
10		0	52.28	74.93	86.23	92.26
11			43.98	70.57	83.84	90.92
12			34.72	65.71	81.17	89.42
13			24.39	60.28	78.19	87.74
14			12.86	54.23	74.86	85.87
15			0	47.47	71.15	83.79
16				39.94	67.01	81.46
17				31.53	62.39	78.87
18				22.15	57.24	75.97
19				11.68	51.49	72.74
20				0	45.08	69.13
21					37.92	65.11
22					29.94	60.63
23					21.03	55.62
24					11.09	50.03
25					0	43.80
26						36.85
27						29.09
28						20.43
29						10.78
30						0

11.25%

Age of Loan	5 years	10 years	15 years	20 years	25 years	30 years
1	84.21	94.26	97.28	98.59	99.23	99.57
2	66.55	87.84	94.25	97.01	98.37	99.10
3	46.80	80.66	90.85	95.24	97.41	98.56
4	24.71	72.63	87.05	93.26	96.34	97.97
5	0	63.64	82.80	91.05	95.14	97.30
6		53.59	78.05	88.58	93.79	96.55
7		42.36	72.73	85.82	92.29	95.72
8		29.79	66.78	82.72	90.61	94.78
9		15.73	60.14	79.26	88.73	93.74
10		0	52.70	75.39	86.63	92.57
11			44.38	71.07	84.27	91.26
12			35.07	66.23	81.64	89.80
13			24.66	60.81	78.70	88.16
14			13.02	54.76	75.41	86.33
15			0	47.98	71.73	84.29
16				40.41	67.61	82.00
17				31.93	63.01	79.44
18				22.46	57.85	76.57
19				11.86	52.09	73.37
20				0	45.65	69.79
21					38.44	65.78
22					30.18	61.30
23					21.36	56.29
24					11.28	50.69
25					0	44.42
26						37.40
27						29.56
28						20.79
29						10.97
30						0

11.50%

Age of Loan	5 years	10 years	15 years	20 years	25 years	30 years
1	84.30	94.34	97.34	98.63	99.26	99.60
2	66.69	87.99	94.37	97.10	98.44	99.14
3	46.95	80.86	91.03	95.38	97.51	98.63
4	24.82	72.88	87.29	93.45	96.48	98.06
5	0	63.93	83.09	91.29	95.32	97.42
6		53.89	78.38	88.87	94.01	96.71
7		42.64	73.11	86.15	92.55	95.90
8		30.02	67.19	83.10	90.91	95.00
9		15.87	60.56	79.68	89.07	93.99
10		0	53.12	75.85	87.01	92.86
11			44.78	71.55	84.70	91.59
12			35.43	66.74	82.11	90.17
13			24.94	61.34	79.21	88.57
14			13.18	55.28	75.95	86.78
15			0	48.49	72.30	84.77
16				40.88	68.20	82.52
17				32.34	63.61	80.00
18				22.77	58.46	77.17
19				12.03	52.69	73.99
20				0	46.22	70.44
21					38.96	66.45
22					30.82	61.97
23					21.70	56.96
24					11.47	51.33
25					0	45.03
26						37.96
27						30.03
28						21.14
29						11.18
30						0

11.75%

Age of Loan	5 years	10 years	15 years	20 years	25 years	30 years
1	84.38	94.41	97.40	98.68	99.30	99.62
2	66.83	88.13	94.20	97.25	98.50	99.19
3	47.10	81.07	91.20	95.51	97.61	98.70
4	24.93	73.13	87.52	93.63	96.61	98.16
5	0	64.21	83.37	91.52	95.49	97.55
6		54.19	78.71	89.14	94.22	96.86
7		42.92	73.48	86.47	92.80	96.09
8		30.25	67.59	83.47	91.20	95.22
9		16.01	60.97	80.09	89.41	94.24
10		0	53.54	76.30	87.39	93.14
11			45.18	72.04	85.12	91.91
12			35.78	67.25	82.57	90.52
13			25.22	61.86	79.70	88.97
14			13.35	55.80	76.48	87.21
15			0	49.00	72.86	85.24
16				41.35	68.79	83.03
17				32.75	64.21	80.54
18				23.08	59.07	77.75
19				12.21	53.28	74.60
20				0	46.78	71.07
21					39.48	67.10
22					31.27	62.63
23					22.04	57.62
24					11.66	51.98
25					0	45.64
26						38.51
27						30.50
28						21.50
29						11.38
30						0

12.00%

Age of Loan	5 years	10 years	15 years	20 years	25 years	30 years
1	84.47	94.49	97.46	98.72	99.32	99.64
2	66.97	88.27	94.60	97.27	98.56	99.23
3	47.25	81.27	91.38	95.65	97.71	98.77
4	25.04	73.39	87.75	93.81	96.74	98.25
5	0	64.50	83.65	91.74	95.65	97.66
6		54.48	79.04	89.42	94.43	97.00
7		43.20	73.84	86.79	93.05	96.26
8		30.48	67.99	83.83	91.49	95.42
9		16.15	61.39	80.50	89.73	94.48
10		0	53.95	76.75	87.76	93.42
11			45.58	72.52	85.53	92.22
12			36.13	67.75	83.02	90.87
13			25.50	62.37	80.19	89.35
14			13.51	56.32	77.00	87.64
15			0	49.50	73.41	85.71
16				41.81	69.36	83.53
17				33.15	64.80	81.08
18				23.39	59.66	78.32
19				12.39	53.87	75.20
20				0	47.35	71.69
21					40.00	67.74
22					31.71	63.29
23					22.37	58.27
24					11.85	52.61
25					0	46.24
26						39.06
27						30.97
28						21.85
29						11.58
30						0

12.25%

Age of Loan	5 years	10 years	15 years	20 years	25 years	30 years
1	84.56	94.56	97.52	98.76	99.35	99.66
2	67.11	88.42	94.71	97.36	98.62	99.27
3	47.41	81.48	91.55	95.77	97.80	98.83
4	25.15	73.64	87.97	93.99	96.87	98.33
5	0	64.78	83.93	91.96	95.81	97.77
6		54.78	79.36	89.68	94.63	97.14
7		43.48	74.21	87.10	93.28	96.43
8		30.71	68.38	84.19	91.76	95.62
9		16.29	61.80	80.90	90.05	94.71
10		0	54.37	77.19	88.12	93.68
11			45.49	72.99	85.93	92.52
12			36.49	68.24	83.46	91.21
13			25.77	62.89	80.67	89.72
14			13.67	56.84	77.52	88.05
15			0	50.00	73.95	86.15
16				42.28	69.93	84.02
17				33.56	65.39	81.60
18				23.70	60.26	78.87
19				12.57	54.46	75.79
20				0	47.91	72.31
21					40.51	68.38
22					32.15	63.93
23					22.71	58.91
24					12.05	53.25
25					0	46.84
26						39.61
27						31.44
28						22.21
29						11.78
30						0

12.50%

Age of Loan	5 years	10 years	15 years	20 years	25 years	30 years
1	84.64	94.63	97.57	98.80	99.38	99.67
2	67.25	88.68	94.83	97.44	98.68	99.31
3	47.56	81.68	91.72	95.90	97.89	98.89
4	25.26	73.89	88.19	94.16	96.99	98.42
5	0	65.06	84.20	92.18	95.97	97.88
6		55.07	79.68	89.94	94.82	97.28
7		43.75	74.57	87.41	93.51	96.59
8		30.94	68.77	84.54	92.03	95.81
9		16.43	62.21	81.30	90.36	94.93
10		0	54.78	77.62	88.47	93.94
11			46.37	73.45	86.32	92.81
12			36.84	68.74	83.89	91.53
13			26.05	63.40	81.14	90.08
14			13.84	57.35	78.02	88.45
15			0	50.50	74.49	86.59
16				42.74	70.49	84.49
17				33.96	65.97	82.11
18				24.02	60.84	79.42
19				12.75	55.04	76.37
20				0	48.46	72.91
21					41.02	69.00
22					32.59	64.57
23					23.05	59.55
24					12.24	53.87
25					0	47.44
26						40.15
27						31.90
28						22.56
29						11.98
30						0

12.75%

Age of Loan	5 years	10 years	15 years	20 years	25 years	30 years
1	84.73	94.71	97.63	98.84	99.41	99.69
2	67.71	88.70	94.94	97.52	98.73	99.34
3	47.71	81.88	91.88	96.02	97.97	98.95
4	25.36	74.13	88.41	94.32	97.10	98.50
5	0	65.34	84.47	92.39	96.12	97.98
6		55.36	80.00	90.20	95.00	97.40
7		44.03	74.93	87.71	93.74	96.74
8		31.17	69.16	84.89	92.30	96.00
9		16.57	62.62	81.68	90.66	95.15
10		0	55.20	78.04	88.81	94.18
11			46.77	73.91	86.70	93.09
12			37.20	69.22	84.31	91.85
13			26.33	63.90	81.60	90.44
14			14.00	57.86	78.51	88.83
15			0	51.00	75.02	87.02
16				43.21	71.05	84.95
17				34.37	66.54	82.61
18				24.33	61.42	79.95
19				12.94	55.61	76.93
20				0	49.02	73.50
21					41.53	69.61
22					33.03	65.20
23					23.39	60.18
24					12.43	54.49
25					0	48.03
26						40.69
27						32.37
28						22.91
29						12.18
30						0

APPENDIX C: Loan Progress Chart: Table Of Remaining Balances

13.00%

Age of Loan	5 years	10 years	15 years	20 years	25 years	30 years
1	84.81	94.78	97.68	98.88	99.43	99.71
2	67.53	88.84	95.04	97.60	98.79	99.38
3	47.86	82.08	92.04	96.14	98.05	99.00
4	25.47	74.38	88.63	94.48	97.22	98.57
5	0	65.62	84.74	92.60	96.27	98.08
6		55.66	80.31	90.45	95.18	97.53
7		44.31	75.28	88.01	93.95	96.89
8		31.41	69.55	85.23	92.55	96.17
9		16.72	63.03	82.07	90.96	95.35
10		0	55.61	78.47	89.14	94.42
11			47.16	74.37	87.07	93.36
12			37.55	69.71	84.72	92.15
13			26.61	64.40	82.05	90.78
14			14.17	58.36	79.00	89.21
15			0	51.49	75.54	87.43
16				43.67	71.59	85.40
17				34.77	67.10	83.10
18				24.64	62.00	80.47
19				13.12	56.18	77.49
20				0	49.57	74.09
21					42.04	70.22
22					33.47	65.82
23					23.72	60.81
24					12.63	55.11
25					0	48.62
26						41.23
27						32.83
28						23.27
29						12.39
30						0

13.25%

Age of Loan	5 years	10 years	15 years	20 years	25 years	30 years
1	84.90	94.85	97.73	98.91	99.46	99.72
2	67.67	88.97	95.15	97.67	98.84	99.41
3	48.01	82.27	92.20	96.26	98.13	99.05
4	25.58	74.62	88.84	94.64	97.33	98.64
5	0	65.90	85.00	92.80	96.41	98.18
6		55.95	80.62	90.70	95.36	97.64
7		44.59	75.63	88.30	94.16	97.03
8		31.64	69.93	85.56	92.80	96.34
9		16.86	63.43	82.44	91.24	95.55
10		0	56.02	78.88	89.46	94.65
11			47.56	74.82	87.44	93.62
12			37.90	70.18	85.13	92.44
13			26.89	64.90	82.49	91.10
14			14.33	58.86	79.48	89.58
15			0	51.98	76.05	87.83
16				44.13	72.13	85.84
17				35.18	67.66	83.57
18				24.96	62.56	80.98
19				13.30	56.75	78.03
20				0	50.12	74.66
21					42.55	70.81
22					33.91	66.43
23					24.06	61.42
24					12.82	55.71
25					0	49.20
26						41.77
27						33.29
28						23.62
29						12.59
30						0

13.50%

Age of Loan	5 years	10 years	15 years	20 years	25 years	30 years
1	84.98	94.92	97.79	98.95	99.48	99.74
2	67.81	89.11	95.26	97.74	98.89	99.44
3	48.16	82.47	92.36	96.37	98.21	99.10
4	25.69	74.87	89.05	94.80	97.43	98.71
5	0	66.18	85.26	93.00	96.54	98.26
6		56.24	80.93	90.94	95.53	97.75
7		44.87	75.98	88.58	94.37	97.17
8		31.87	70.31	85.89	93.04	96.50
9		17.00	63.83	82.81	91.52	95.74
10		0	56.42	79.29	89.78	94.87
11			47.95	75.26	87.79	93.87
12			38.26	70.66	85.52	92.73
13			27.17	65.39	82.92	91.42
14			14.50	59.36	79.95	89.93
15			0	52.47	76.55	88.22
16				44.59	72.66	86.27
17				35.58	68.21	84.04
18				25.27	63.13	81.48
19				13.48	57.31	78.56
20				0	50.66	75.22
21					43.05	71.40
22					34.35	67.03
23					24.40	62.03
24					13.02	56.32
25					0	49.78
26						42.30
27						33.75
28						23.97
29						12.79
30						0

13.75%

Age of Loan	5 years	10 years	15 years	20 years	25 years	30 years
1	85.07	94.99	97.84	98.98	99.50	99.75
2	67.94	89.25	95.36	97.82	98.93	99.47
3	48.31	82.66	92.51	96.48	98.28	99.15
4	25.80	75.11	89.26	94.95	97.53	98.78
5	0	66.45	85.52	93.19	96.68	98.35
6		56.53	81.23	91.17	95.69	97.86
7		45.15	76.32	88.86	94.56	97.30
8		32.11	70.69	86.21	93.27	96.66
9		17.15	64.23	83.17	91.79	95.92
10		0	56.83	79.69	90.09	95.08
11			48.34	75.70	88.14	94.11
12			38.61	71.12	85.91	93.00
13			27.46	65.87	83.35	91.73
14			14.66	59.86	80.41	90.27
15			0	52.96	77.04	88.60
16				45.05	73.18	86.69
17				35.98	68.76	84.49
18				25.59	63.68	81.97
19				13.67	57.87	79.08
20				0	51.20	75.77
21					43.55	71.98
22					34.79	67.62
23					24.73	62.63
24					11.21	56.91
25					0	50.35
26						42.83
27						34.21
28						24.33
29						12.99
30						0

14.00%

Age of Loan	5 years	10 years	15 years	20 years	25 years	30 years
1	85.15	95.06	97.89	99.02	99.53	99.77
2	68.08	89.38	95.56	97.89	99.02	99.50
3	48.46	82.85	92.67	96.59	98.35	99.19
4	25.91	75.35	89.46	95.09	97.80	98.84
5	0	66.73	85.77	93.38	96.80	98.43
6		56.82	81.53	91.40	95.85	97.96
7		45.43	76.66	89.13	94.76	97.43
8		32.34	71.06	86.53	93.50	96.81
9		17.29	64.63	83.53	92.05	96.10
10		0	57.23	80.09	90.39	95.28
11			48.73	76.13	88.48	94.35
12			38.97	71.58	86.28	93.27
13			27.74	66.36	83.76	92.03
14			14.83	60.35	80.86	90.61
15			0	53.44	77.53	88.97
16				45.51	73.70	87.09
17				36.38	69.30	84.93
18				25.90	64.23	82.45
19				13.85	58.42	79.59
20				0	51.73	76.31
21					44.05	72.54
22					35.22	68.21
23					25.07	63.23
24					13.41	57.50
25					0	50.92
26						43.36
27						34.67
28						24.68
29						13.20
30						0

14.25%

Age of Loan	5 years	10 years	15 years	20 years	25 years	30 years
1	85.23	95.13	97.94	99.05	99.55	99.78
2	68.22	89.51	95.56	97.95	99.02	99.53
3	48.61	83.04	92.82	96.69	98.42	99.23
4	26.03	75.59	89.66	95.24	97.73	98.90
5	0	67.00	86.02	93.56	96.93	98.51
6		57.11	81.83	91.63	96.00	98.06
7		45.71	77.00	89.40	94.94	97.55
8		32.57	71.44	86.84	93.72	96.95
9		17.44	65.02	83.88	92.31	96.27
10		0	57.64	80.48	90.68	95.48
11			49.12	76.56	88.81	94.57
12			39.32	72.04	86.65	93.53
13			28.02	66.83	84.17	92.32
14			15.00	60.84	81.31	90.93
15			0	53.92	78.01	89.33
16				45.96	74.21	87.49
17				36.79	69.83	85.36
18				26.21	64.78	82.91
19				14.03	58.97	80.09
20				0	52.27	76.84
21					44.55	73.10
22					35.65	68.78
23					25.41	63.81
24					13.60	58.09
25					0	51.49
26						43.88
27						35.12
28						25.03
29						13.40
30						0

14.50%

Age of Loan	5 years	10 years	15 years	20 years	25 years	30 years
1	85.32	95.19	97.98	99.08	99.57	99.79
2	68.35	89.64	95.65	98.02	99.06	99.55
3	48.76	83.23	92.96	96.79	98.49	99.27
4	26.14	75.83	89.86	95.37	97.82	98.95
5	0	67.28	86.27	93.74	97.04	98.58
6		57.40	82.12	91.85	96.15	98.15
7		45.99	77.33	89.66	95.12	97.66
8		32.81	71.80	87.14	93.93	97.09
9		17.58	65.42	84.23	92.56	96.43
10		0	58.04	80.87	90.97	95.67
11			49.51	76.98	89.13	94.79
12			39.67	72.49	87.01	93.77
13			28.30	67.31	84.57	92.60
14			15.17	61.32	81.74	91.24
15			0	54.40	78.48	89.68
16				46.41	74.70	87.87
17				37.19	70.35	85.78
18				26.53	65.32	83.37
19				14.22	59.51	80.58
20				0	52.79	77.36
21					45.04	73.65
22					36.09	69.35
23					25.74	64.39
24					13.80	58.66
25					0	52.05
26						44.40
27						35.58
28						25.38
29						13.60
30						0

14.75%

Age of Loan	5 years	10 years	15 years	20 years	25 years	30 years
1	85.40	95.26	98.03	99.11	99.59	99.80
2	68.49	89.77	95.75	98.08	99.10	99.58
3	48.91	83.42	93.11	96.89	98.55	99.31
4	26.25	76.06	90.05	95.51	97.90	99.01
5	0	67.55	86.51	93.91	97.16	98.65
6		57.68	82.41	92.06	96.30	98.24
7		46.26	77.66	89.92	95.30	97.77
8		33.04	72.17	87.44	94.14	97.22
9		17.73	65.80	84.57	92.80	96.59
10		0	58.43	81.24	91.24	95.85
11			49.90	77.39	89.45	95.00
12			40.02	72.94	87.37	94.01
13			28.58	67.78	84.96	92.87
14			15.34	61.80	82.17	91.55
15			0	54.88	78.94	90.02
16				46.86	75.20	88.24
17				37.59	70.86	86.19
18				26.84	65.85	83.81
19				14.40	60.04	81.06
20				0	53.32	77.87
21					45.53	74.18
22					36.52	69.91
23					26.08	64.96
24					13.99	59.23
25					0	52.60
26						44.92
27						36.03
28						25.73
29						13.81
30						0

APPENDIX C: Loan Progress Chart: Table Of Remaining Balances

15.00%

Age of Loan	5 years	10 years	15 years	20 years	25 years	30 years
1	85.48	95.33	98.08	99.14	99.60	99.81
2	68.63	89.90	95.94	98.14	99.14	99.60
3	49.06	83.61	93.25	96.99	98.61	99.35
4	26.36	76.30	90.24	95.64	97.99	99.06
5	0	67.82	86.75	94.08	97.27	98.72
6		57.97	82.70	92.27	96.43	98.33
7		46.54	77.99	90.17	95.46	97.87
8		33.27	72.53	87.73	94.34	97.35
9		17.87	66.19	84.90	93.03	96.74
10		0	58.83	81.62	91.51	96.02
11			50.29	77.80	89.75	95.20
12			40.37	73.38	87.71	94.24
13			28.87	68.24	85.14	93.13
14			15.51	62.27	82.59	91.84
15			0	55.35	79.39	90.34
16				47.31	75.68	88.61
17				37.99	71.37	86.59
18				27.16	66.38	84.25
19				14.59	60.57	81.53
20				0	53.84	78.37
21					46.02	74.71
22					36.95	70.46
23					26.42	65.53
24					14.19	59.80
25					0	53.15
26						45.43
27						36.48
28						26.08
29						14.01
30						0

15.25%

Age of Loan	5 years	10 years	15 years	20 years	25 years	30 years
1	85.56	95.39	98.12	99.17	99.62	99.82
2	68.76	90.03	95.94	98.20	99.18	99.62
3	49.22	83.79	93.39	97.08	98.67	99.38
4	26.47	76.53	90.43	95.77	98.07	99.11
5	0	68.09	86.99	94.25	97.38	98.78
6		58.26	82.98	92.48	96.57	98.41
7		46.82	78.32	90.42	95.63	97.98
8		33.51	72.89	88.02	94.53	97.47
9		18.02	66.57	85.23	93.26	96.88
10		0	59.23	81.99	91.78	96.19
11			50.67	78.21	90.05	95.39
12			40.73	73.81	88.05	94.47
13			29.15	68.70	85.71	93.38
14			15.68	62.75	83.00	92.13
15			0	55.82	79.83	90.66
16				47.76	76.16	88.96
17				38.38	71.88	86.98
18				27.47	66.90	84.67
19				14.77	61.10	81.99
20				0	54.36	78.86
21					46.51	75.23
22					37.38	71.00
23					26.75	66.08
24					14.39	60.36
25					0	53.70
26						45.94
27						36.92
28						26.43
29						14.21
30						0

15.50%

Age of Loan	5 years	10 years	15 years	20 years	25 years	30 years
1	85.64	95.46	98.17	99.20	99.64	99.83
2	68.90	90.16	96.03	98.26	99.22	99.64
3	49.37	83.98	93.53	97.17	98.72	99.42
4	26.58	76.76	90.62	95.90	98.15	99.15
5	0	68.35	87.22	94.41	97.48	98.85
6		58.54	83.26	92.68	96.70	98.49
7		47.09	78.64	90.66	95.79	98.07
8		33.74	73.24	88.30	94.72	97.58
9		18.17	66.95	85.55	93.48	97.02
10		0	59.62	82.35	92.03	96.35
11			51.06	78.61	90.34	95.58
12			41.08	74.24	88.38	94.68
13			29.43	69.15	86.08	93.63
14			15.85	63.21	83.40	92.40
15			0	56.29	80.27	90.97
16				48.21	76.62	89.30
17				38.78	72.37	87.36
18				27.79	67.41	85.08
19				14.96	61.62	82.44
20				0	54.87	79.35
21					46.99	75.74
22					37.80	71.54
23					27.09	66.63
24					14.58	60.91
25					0	54.23
26						46.45
27						37.37
28						26.77
29						14.42
30						0

Appendix D
GLOSSARY OF REAL ESTATE TERMS

Abstract of Title	A short history of a piece of property, tracing its chain of ownership (title) through the years, plus a record of all liens, taxes, judgments or other encumbrances that may impair the title. Your title insurance company reviews the abstract to make sure the title comes to a buyer free of any defects (problems).
Acceleration Clause	A provision in a mortgage or trust deed that may require the unpaid balance of the mortgage loan to become due immediately, if the regular mortgage payments are not made, or if other terms of the mortgage are not met.
Access Right	The right of an owner or lessee to freely go to and from his or her property.
Accord & Satisfaction	An agreement or a document settling a claim or a suit.
Acknowledgment	A declaration before a person qualified under the law to administer oaths, to the effect that a document or a deed is the act of the person who signed it.
Acre ft.).	A piece of land measuring 43,560 square feet (i.e., about 208.71 ft. by 208.71
Act of God	An accident which could not have been foreseen or prevented, such as those caused by earthquakes, severe storms, and the like.
Ad Valorem	A latin phrase meaning "according to value."
Advance Commitment	A written offer by a lender to make a mortgage loan at a stated interest rate over a specific number of years.
Adverse Possession	The physical occupancy or possession of property in spite of, and in defiance of, someone else's legal title. If such possession continues for twenty years, legal title can be claimed by the one in possession.
Affidavit	A written statement, sworn to before a notary public or other officer authorized to administer oaths.
Agreement of Sale	A contract between seller and purchaser stating the terms and conditions of sale. (See also Purchase Agreement)
Alienation	The transfer of property from one person to another.
Amortization	A method of paying off the principal owed on a loan in regular installments (as opposed to making the entire payment in one lump sum on a certain date).
Appraisal	An estimate of the market value of a home—that is, what it would sell for under normal conditions. 'Market value' is almost never the same as replacement cost, so an appraisal made by a lender is not adequate for insurance purposes.

Appraiser
house.

A professional who charges to estimate the market or replacement value of a

Appreciation

An increase in the value of a piece of property, not including the added value of the property made by extensions and improvements. A property may appreciate in dollar value simply because of inflation, or in real value because of limited housing availability, improved neighborhoods, etc.

Assessed Value

The value of a property as determined by the tax assessor for the purpose of collecting property taxes. The assessed value is usually a fixed percentage of either the market value or the most recent purchase price.

Assessment

A special tax due for a special purpose and charged to a specific group of homeowners who are benefiting from a municipal improvement (for example, a sewer tax, street tax, etc.); may also refer to the value placed on property for purpose of taxation.

Assumption of Mortgage

The promise by the buyer of property to be legally responsible for the payment of an existing mortgage. The purchaser's name is substituted for the original mortgagor's (borrower's) name on the mortgage note and the original mortgagor is released from the responsibility of making the mortgage payments. Usually the lender must agree to an assumption.

Attachment

The seizure of property by court order.

Balloon Payment

When the final payment on an installment loan is larger than the preceding payments and it pays the debt in full, it is called a balloon payment.

Bench Mark

A permanent marker placed in the ground by the city to help surveyors establish property lines. Also known as a 'monument.'

Binder

A simple contract between a buyer and a seller which states the basic terms of an offer to purchase property. It is usually good only for a limited period of time, until a more formal purchase agreement is prepared and signed by both parties.

Blanket Mortgage

A simple mortgage which covers several pieces of real estate.

(Real Estate) Broker

A person licensed by the state to arrange the purchase or sale of land or real property, acting as intermediary between buyer and seller, and often between buyer and lender. Also known as a real estate agent.

Buy-down

See p. 163 of the manual.

Carrying Charges

What it actually costs for a homeowner to maintain his home—including the mortgage payments, taxes, and general maintenance.

Certificate of Title

A written opinion by an attorney that his examination of land records has established a clear ownership of property.

Chattel Mortgage

The creation of a loan on personal property as security for payment on a real estate loan.

Chattels

Goods, or any other type of property, which are not real property (real property generally includes land, and whatever is erected or growing upon it).

Closing

The final step in the sale and purchase of a property, when the title is transferred from the seller to the buyer; the buyer signs the mortgage, pays the settlement costs; and any money due the seller or buyer is handed over.

Closing Costs	The various expenses, over and above the actual sale price of the property, involved in arranging a real estate transfer.
Cloud on the Title	Any condition which may affect the title to property, usually a minor matter which can be settled with a quitclaim deed or court judgment. (See Title Defect)
Commission	A real estate agent's or broker's compensation for his services, usually a percentage of the selling price or rental and is spelled out in the Purchase (Sales') Agreement.
Community Property	In some states, a form of ownership under which property acquired during a marriage is presumed to be owned jointly unless acquired as separate property of either spouse.
Conditional Commitment credit rating.	A promise to insure (generally with FHA loans) payment of a definite loan amount on a particular piece of property for a buyer with a satisfactory
Condominium	Individual ownership of an apartment in a multi-unit project or development, and a proportionate interest in the common areas outside the apartment.
Contractor	A person or company who agrees to furnish materials and labor to do work for a certain price.
Conventional Loan	A mortgage loan which is not insured by FHA or guaranteed by VA.
Conveyance	The transfer of the title (that is, evidence of ownership) of property by deed from one person to another.
Cooperative (Apartment)	An apartment building or group of housing units owned by all the residents (generally a corporation) and run by an elected board of directors for the benefit of the residents. The resident lives in his unit but does not own it—he owns a share of stock in the corporation.
Covenant	A promise or agreement between two parties usually applied to specific promises in a deed.
Credit Rating	A rating or evaluation made of one's financial standing by a person or company (such as a Credit Bureau), based on one's present financial condition and past credit history.
Credit Report	A report usually ordered by a lender from a credit bureau to help determine a borrower's credit rating.
Deed	A written document by which the ownership of property is transferred from the seller (the grantor) to the buyer (the grantee).
Deed of Trust	In some states, generally those west of the Mississippi River, a document used instead of a mortgage. It transfers title of the property to a third party (the trustee) who holds the title until the debt or mortgage loan is fully repaid to the lender, at which time the title (ownership) passes to the borrower. If the borrower defaults (fails to make payments), the trustee may sell the property at a public sale to pay off the loan.
Deed (Quitclaim Deed)	A deed which transfers only that title or right to a property, if any, that the holder of that title has at the time of the transfer. A quitclaim deed does not warrant (or guarantee) a clear or definite title.
Deed (Warranty Deed)	A deed which guarantees that the title to a piece of property is free from any title defects.

Default	Failure to make mortgage payments on time, as agreed to in the mortgage note or deed of trust. Generally, if a payment is 30 days late, the mortgage is technically in default, and it may give the lender the right to start foreclosure proceedings.
Defeasance Clause	The clause in a mortgage which gives the borrower the right to regain clear ownership of his property upon full payment of his obligation to the lender.
Defect of Record	Any lien or encumbrance upon a title which is part of the public record.
Delinquency	The state of a mortgage payment being past due.
Deposit	A sum of money given to bind a sale of real estate—also called 'earnest money.'
Depreciation	A loss or decrease in the value of a piece of property due to age, wear and tear, or unfavorable changes in the neighborhood; opposite of appreciation.
Discount	The difference between the normal dollar amount of a loan and the lesser amount which is actually given to the borrower. This difference is usually charged in "points" to the borrower.
Documentary Stamps	In some states a tax, in the form of stamps, required on deeds and mortgages when real estate title passes from one owner to another. The amount required differs from one state to another.
Down Payment	The money a buyer must pay in cash on a house before being granted a loan.
"Due on Sale" clause	A provision often stipulated in a mortgage loan contract, which gives the lender the right and option to require full and immediate repayment of the entire balance you still owed on the loan—at any future time when you ever sell or transfer the property. Here's an example of a typical due-on-sale clause: "If all or any part of the property or an interest therein is sold or transferred by Borrower without Lender's prior written consent.... Lender may, at Lender's option, declare all the sums secured by this Mortgage to be immediately due and payable."
Earnest Money	(See Deposit)
Easement	The right to use land owned by another. For instance, the electric company has easement rights to allow their power lines to cross another's property.
ECOA	Equal Credit Opportunity Act—a federal law that requires lenders to loan without discrimination based on race, color, religion, national origin, sex, marital status, or income from public assistance programs.
Eminent Domain	The government's right to acquire property for necessary public or quasi-public use.
Enroachment	The building of a structure or improvements which trespass on the property of another person.
Encumbrance	Anything that limits the interest in a title to property, such as a mortgage, a lien, an easement, a deed restriction, or unpaid taxes.
Equity	A buyer's initial ownership interest in a house and the increases thereof as he pays off a mortgage loan. When the mortgage is fully paid, the owner has 100% equity in his house.
Equity of Redemption	The right of an owner to regain his or her property during a foreclosure action for nonpayment.
Escalation Clause	A clause in a contract which allows the adjustment of certain items (such as the size of a monthly mortgage payment) in certain circumstances.
Escrow	Money or documents held by a neutral third party until all or certain specified conditions of a contract are met.

Escrow Agent	The third party responsible to the buyer and seller or to the lender and borrower for holding the money or documents until the terms of a purchase agreement are met.
Escrow Payment	That part of a borrower's monthly payment held by the lender to pay for taxes, hazard insurance, mortgage insurance, and other items until they become due. Also known as **'impounds'** or **'reserves'** in some states.
Exclusive Agency Listing	A document giving one agent the right to sell a piece of property for a certain period of time, but reserving the right of the owner to sell the property himself without paying a commission.
Exclusive 'Right to Sell' Listing	A document which gives an agent the right to collect a commission if the property is sold by anyone during the term of the agreement, regardless of who found the buyer.
Fee Simple	The most complete ownership of land, one without any known limitations on the owner's right to dispose of the property as he or she chooses.
FHA	Federal Housing Administration—a division of the U.S. Department of Housing and Urban Development (HUD). Its main activity is to insure home mortgage loans made by private lenders.
FmHA	Farmers Home Administration—a government agency (part of the Department of Agriculture) which provides financing to farmers or other qualified buyers (usually in rural areas) who are unable to obtain loans elsewhere.
Finance Charge	The total of all charges one must pay in order to get a loan.
Firm Commitment	An agreement from a lender to make a loan to a particular borrower on a particular property. Also an FHA or private mortgage insurance company agreement to insure a loan on a particular property for a particular borrower.
Forbearance	The act of delaying legal action to foreclose on a mortgage that is overdue. Usually it is granted only when a satisfactory arrangement has been made with the lender to make up the late payments at a future date.
Foreclosure	The legal process by which a lender forces payment of a loan (under a mortgage or deed of trust) by taking the property from the owner (mortgagor) and selling it to pay off the debt.
Grantee	That party in the deed who is the buyer.
Grantor	That party in the deed who is the seller.
Guaranteed Loan	A loan guaranteed to be paid by the VA or FMHA in the event the borrower fails to do so (defaults).
Guaranty	A promise by one person to pay the debt of another if that other person fails to do so.
Hazard Insurance	Insurance which protects against damage caused to property by fire, windstorm, or other common hazard. Required by many lenders to be carried in an amount at least equal to the mortgage.
Hidden Defect	Any encumbrance on a title that is not given in the public record (e.g., unknown liens, forged documents, etc.).
HUD	The U.S. Department of Housing and Urban Development.
Impound	(See Escrow)

Installment	The regular payment that a borrower agrees to make to a lender on or by specified dates.
Instrument	A written legal document.
Insurance Binder	A document stating that an individual or property is insured, even though the insurance policy has not yet been issued.
Insured Loan	A loan insured by FHA or a private mortgage insurance company.
Interest	A charge paid for borrowing money, usually set as a percentage of the amount borrowed. Also used to refer to a right, share or title in property.
Joint Tenancy	An equal, undivided ownership of property by two or more persons. Should one of the parties die, his share of the ownership would pass to the surviving owners (right of survivorship).
Land Contract	A sales contract which allows the seller to retain title to the property until the buyer has paid the full purchase price.
Late Charge	An additional fee a lender charges a borrower if his mortgage payments are not made on time.
Lien	A hold or claim which someone has on the property of another as security for a debt or charge; if a lien is not removed (if debt is not paid) , the property may be sold to pay off the lien.
Life Estate	Taking ownership of property for the lifetime of a given person (a "life estate"), after which the property goes, after the first person dies, to another designated person; an estate (property) meant for the use or enjoyment of the designated beneficiary only for the lifetime of the person.
Listing	Registering of property for sale with one or more real estate brokers or agents allowing the broker who actually sells the property to get the commission.
Loan Disclosure Note	Document spelling out all the terms involved in obtaining and paying off a loan.
Margin of Security	The difference between the amount of the mortgage loan(s) and the appraised value of the property.
Market Value	The amount of money that serious prospective buyers are likely to offer to pay for a piece of property at a given time.
Marketable Title	A title clear of any encumbrances or objectionable liens that might adversely affect an owner's ability to sell.
Mechanic's Lien	A lien which building contractors, suppliers, and workmen are allowed by state law to invoke for unpaid bills.
Monument	A fixed object established by surveyors to mark land locations.
Mortgage	A loan given especially for the purpose of buying real property; a lien on real property which home owner (borrower) gives his lender as security for the borrowed money.
Mortgage Interest Subsidy	A monthly payment by the Federal Government to a mortgagee (lender) which reduces the amount of interest the mortgagor (homeowner) has to pay to lender to as low as 4%, if the homeowner falls within certain income limits.
Mortgage Origination Fee	A charge by the lender for the work involved in the preparation and servicing of a mortgage request. Usually 1 percent of the loan amount.
Mortgagee	The lender who makes a mortgage loan.
Mortgagor	The person borrowing money for a mortgage loan.

Multiple Listing	A system in which a group of brokers (as opposed to one broker) have a right to sell a property which has been exclusively listed with them. The broker who had the original right to sell receives a portion of the commission if one of the others sells the property.
Net Listing	A listing arrangement which allows a broker to keep as compensation all sums received above a net price.
Note	A written and signed document in which a borrower acknowledges a debt and promises repayment.
Offset Statement	A statement by an owner of property listing the present status of all liens against that property.
Open-end Mortgage	A mortgage which allows a borrower to borrow additional money at a later time without paying the usual financing charges.
Open Listing	An arrangement which gives a broker the non-exclusive right to sell an owner's property. Open listings may be given to several agents and only the agent that sells the home is entitled to a commission.
Option (to buy)	An agreement granting a potential buyer the right to buy a piece of property at a stated price within a stated period of time.
Perfecting Title	The elimination of all claims against a title by payment or court judgment.
PITI	Principal, interest, taxes, and insurance (in FHA and VA loans paid to the bank each month).
Plat (or plot)	A map of a piece of land showing its boundaries, length, width and any easements.
Point(s)	An amount equal to 1% of the principal amount of a loan. Points are a one-time charge collected by the lender at closing to increase his return on the loan. In FHA or VA loans, the borrower himself is allowed to pay only a limited and designated number of points.
Prepaid Items	An advance payment, at the time of closing, for taxes, hazard insurance, and mortgage insurance, which is held in an escrow account by the lender.
Prepayment Penalty	A charge made by the lender if a mortgage loan is paid off before the due date. FHA does not permit such a penalty on its FHA-insured loans.
Principal	The amount of money itself borrowed, as differentiated from the interest and other finance charges which must be paid back on a loan.
Purchase Agreement	A written document in which a seller agrees to sell, and a buyer agrees to buy a piece of property, with certain conditions and terms of the sale spelled out, such as sales price, date of closing, condition of property, etc. The agreement is secured by a deposit or down payment of earnest money.
Quiet Title	A court action taken to establish title, often used to remove a cloud on the title.
Quitclaim Deed	(See Deed, Quitclaim)
Real Estate	Land and the structures erected or growing upon it. Also anything of a permanent nature such as trees, minerals, and the interest and rights in these items.
Real Estate Agent	An individual who can show property for sale on behalf of a seller, but who may not have a license to transact the sale and collect the sales commission.

Real Estate Broker	(See Broker-Real Estate)
Realtor	A real estate broker or an associate holding active membership in a local real estate board affiliated with the National Association of Realtors.
Recording Fees	The charge payable to a local or county land registry to put on public record the details of legal documents such as a deed or mortgage.
Redemption	Buying back one's property after a court-ordered sale.
Refinancing	The process of paying off one loan with the money (proceeds) from another loan.
RESPA	Real Estate Settlement Procedures Act—A federal law that requires lenders to send to the home mortgage borrower (within 3 business days) an estimate of the closing (settlement) costs. RESPA also limits the amount lenders may hold in an escrow account for real estate taxes and insurance, and requires the disclosure of settlement costs to both buyers and sellers at least 24 hours before the closing.
Restrictions	A legal limitation in the deed on the use of property.
Right of Rescission	That section of the **Truth-in-Lending Law** which allows a customer the right to change his/her mind and cancel a contract within 3 days after signing it. This right to cancel is in force if the contract would involve obtaining a loan, and if the loan would place a lien on the property.
Right of Way	An easement on property, where the property owner gives another person the right to pass over his land.
Sales Agreement	(See Purchase Agreement)
Sale-Leaseback	An arrangement in which the owner of a piece of property sells his land to another but retains the right to continue occupancy as a tenant under a lease.
Secondary Financing	A loan secured by a second mortgage or trust deed.
Security Agreement	The agreement between the lender (the secured party) and the debtor which creates the security interest (see below).
Security Interest	The interest of the creditor in the property of the debtor in any credit transaction.
Section	A piece of land in a government survey which contains 640 acres.
Settlement Costs	(See Closing Costs)
Severalty ownership	Owned by one person only; the sole owner.
Sheriff's Deed	A deed granted by a court as part of the forced sale of property (foreclosure) to satisfy a judgment.
Stamps	(See Documentary Stamps)
Subordination Clause	A clause in a second lien which recognizes the priority of prior (first) liens. First liens often have subordination clauses allowing prior claims by mechanic's liens.
Surety	One who guarantees the performance of another: a guarantor.
Survey	A map or plat made by a licensed surveyor showing the measurements of a piece of land; its location, dimensions, and the location and dimensions of any improvements on the land.
Tax Sale	The sale of property for non-payment of taxes.
Tenancy-by-the-Entirety	The joint ownership of property by a husband and wife in such a manner that if either one dies, his or her share of ownership goes to the remaining survivor.

Tenancy-in-Common	When property is owned by two or more persons with the terms creating a joint tenancy, but in such a manner that in the event one of the owners dies, his share of the property would not go to the other surviving owner automatically, but rather to his (the decedent's own) heirs.
Title	The rights of ownership of a particular property, and the documents which prove that ownership (commonly a deed).
Title Defects	An outstanding claim or encumbrance on property which affects its marketability (whether or not it can be freely sold).
Title Insurance	Special Insurance which usually protects lenders against loss of their interest in property due to legal defects in the title. An owner can protect his interest by purchasing separate coverage.
Title Search	An examination of public records to uncover any past or current facts regarding the ownership of a piece of property. A title search is intended to make sure the title is marketable and free from defects.
Truth-in-Lending	A federal law which provides that the terms of a loan (including all the finance charges) must be disclosed to the borrower before the loan is signed. It also contains a provision for the Right of Rescission.
Trust Deed	(See Deed of Trust)
Trustee tion.	One who holds property in trust for another to secure the performance of an obliga-
Trustor	One who deeds his property to a trustee.
VA	Veterans Administration—The VA guarantees a certain proportion of a mortgage loan made to a veteran by a private lender. Sometimes called GI loans, these usually require very low down payments and permit long repayment terms.
Valuation	Estimated worth or price.
Vendee	A buyer.
Vendor	A seller.
Void	To have no effect; something that is unenforceable.
Waive	To relinquish a right to enforce or require something.
Warranty Deed	(See Deed, Warranty)
Wraparound Mortgage	A secondary mortgage arrangement in which the home buyer reimburses the seller for the seller's continuing pay off of his mortgage (presumably at a lower interest rate than would currently by available to the buyer).
Zoning	The legal power of a local municipal government (city or town) to regulate the use of property within the municipality.

Appendix E
Some Relevant Bibliography

Shaun Aghili, *The No-Nonsense Credit Manual* (I.L.S. Publishing, Irvine CA: 1998)

William R. Allen, *New York Real Esate Practices* (National Real Estate Institute, Redmond, Washington)

American Homeowners Foundation, *How To Sell Your Home Fast* (Arlington, VA)

Harley Bjelland, *How To Sell Your House Without A Broker* (Cornerstone Library, N.Y. 1979)

David Crank, *Godly Finances:The Bible Way To Pay off Your Home* (David Publications, St. Louis Mo., 1996)

John R. Dorfman, ed., *The Mortgage Book* (Consumer Reports Books, Yonkers, N.Y. 1992)

The Editors of Rodale Press, *Cut Your Spending In Half Without Settling For Less* (Rodale Press, Emmaus, PA: 1994)

Vijay Fadia, *How To Cut Your Mortgage In Half* (Penguin Books, New York: 1990)

Federal Trade Commission, *The Mortgage Money Guide* (Washington, D.C.)

Richard F. Gabriel, *How To Buy Your Own House When You Don't Have Enough Money!* (Signet, New America Library, N.Y. 1982)

Earl C. Gottschalk Jr., "Picking the Wrong Mortgage Broker Can Become A Homeowner's Nightmare." *The Wall Street Journal*, 26 March 1992: C1, C18.

Kiplinger's Personal Finance Magazine, "Selling Your Home Do It Yourself?" (Feb. 1995), p. 86-9.

HALT, *Real Estate* (Washington, D.C.)

HSH Associates, *How To Shop For Your Mortgage* (Butler, N.J. 1989)

Robert Irwin, *The For Sale By Owner Kit* (Dearborn Financial Publishing, Chicago, IL)

Danielle Kennedy, *Double Your Income in Real Estate Sales* (John Wiley & Sons, N.J.)

Andrew J. McLean, *Investing in Real Estate* (John Wiley & Sons, N.J.)

Peter G. Miller, *How To Save Money When You Hire A Real Estate Broker,* (The Springhill Press, Silver Springs, MD)

Robert G. Natelson, *How To Buy and Sell A Condominium* (Simon & Schuster: 1981)

N.Y. Times, "Picking The Best Broker," Sunday Section 10, June 12, 1994; "Your Home: Haggling Do's and Dont's," Sun. Sec. 10, Aug. 7, 1994; "An Appellate Ruling Rekindles Disclosure Debate," Sun., April 24, 1994, Sec. D., p. 9.

Frank R. Pajares, *For Sale By Owner* (New Trend Publication, Tampa, FL)

Pete, Marwick, Mitchell & Co., *RESPA: The 1979-80 Evaluation, Vol. I: Executive Summary* (October 1980)

Alex Rachun, *How To Inspect The Older House* (N.Y. State College of Human Ecology, Cornell University, N.Y.)

Robert Schwartz, *The Home Owner's Legal Guide* (Collier, Macmillan Publishers, N.Y. 1965)

Martin M. Shenkman and Warren Boronson, *How To Sell Your House In A Buyer's Market* (John Wiley & Sons N.Y. 1990)

Michael C. Thomsett, *Save $ On Your Mortgage: The Mortgage Acceleration Techniques* (John Wiley & Sons: 1989)

Michael C. Thomsett, *Your Home Mortgage* (John Wiley & Sons: 1992)

Appendix **F**

LIST OF OTHER PUBLICATIONS FROM
DO-IT-YOURSELF LEGAL PUBLISHERS

Please DO NOT tear our this page. Consider others!

The following is a list of books obtainable from the Do-It-Yourself Publishers/Selfhelper Law Press of America.

(Customers: For your convenience, just make a photocopy of this page and send it along with your order. All prices quoted here are subject to change without notice.)

1. How To Draw Up Your Own Friendly Separation/Property Settlement Agreement With Your Spouse
2. Tenant Smart: How To Win Your Tenants' Legal Rights Without A Lawyer (New York Edition)
3. How To Probate & Settle An Estate Yourself Without The Lawyers' Fees ($35)
4. How To Adopt A Child Without A Lawyer
5. How To Form Your Own Profit/Non-Profit Corporation Without A Lawyer
6. How To Plan Your 'Total' Estate With A Will & Living Will, Without a Lawyer
7. How To Declare Your Personal Bankruptcy Without A Lawyer ($29)
8. How To Buy Or Sell Your Own Home Without A Lawyer or Broker ($29)
9. How To File For Chapter 11 Business Bankruptcy Without A Lawyer ($29)
10. How To Legally Beat The Traffic Ticket Without A Lawyer (forthcoming)
11. How To Settle Your Own Auto Accident Claims Without A Lawyer ($29)
12. How To Obtain Your U.S. Immigration Visa Without A Lawyer ($25)
13. How To Do Your Own Divorce Without A Lawyer [10 Regional State-Specific Volumes] ($35)
14. How To Legally Change Your Name Without A Lawyer
15. How To Properly Plan Your 'Total' Estate With A Living Trust, Without The Lawyers' Fees ($35)
16. Legally Protect Yourself In A Gay/Lesbian Or Non-Marital Relationship With A Cohabitation Agreement
17. Before You Say 'I do' In Marriage Or Co-Habitation, Here's How To First Protect Yourself Legally
18. The National Home Mortgage reduction Kit (forthcoming) ($26.95)

Prices: Each book, except for those specifically priced otherwise, costs $26, plus $4.00 per book for postage and handling. New Jersey residents please add 6% sales tax. **ALL PRICES ARE SUBJECT TO CHANGE WITHOUT NOTICE**

CUSTOMERS: Please make and send a zerox copy of this page with your orders)

ORDER FORM

TO: **Do-it-Yourself Legal Publishers**
60 Park Place # Suite 1013, Newark, NJ 07102

Please send me the following:

1. _____copies of _____
2. _____copies of _____
3. _____copies of _____
4. _____copies of _____

Enclosed is the sum of $_____ to cover the order. *Mail my order to:*
Mr./Mrs.//Ms/Dr. _____
Address (include Zip Code please): _____
_____
Phone No. and area code: ( ) _____ Job: ( ) _____
*New Jersey residents enclose 6% sales tax.

IMPORTANT: Please do NOT rip out the page. Consider others! Just make a photocopy and send it.

INDEX